D1180274

LITTLE BOOK OF
CLIFF RICHARD

LITTLE BOOK OF
CLIFF RICHARD

First published in the UK in 2012

© G2 Entertainment Limited 2012

www.G2ent.co.uk

Printed and bound in China

ISBN 978-1-909217-17-1

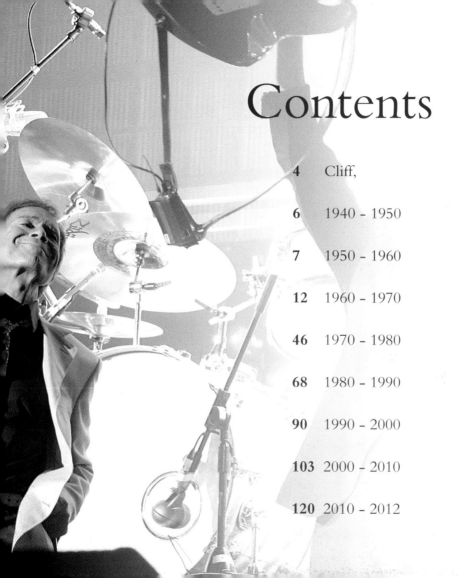

Contents

Cliff,

A heart felt congratulations on 50 years at the top!

It's a privilege to have been a part of it and a pal for the last 30 years, sharing TV and Radio shows, tennis courts, holidays, stages and parties.

Hey! We got to play for, and with, the Princess of Wales and the future King and his brother. Now that's a line-up!

I'm proud as a writer that you recorded three of my songs, More To Life, November Night and the Tsunami single Grief Never Grows Old and was equally proud to be able to give something back by flying Roy Bennett over from the States as a surprise so you could sing The Young Ones together. Who says giving is not as pleasurable as receiving!

It was also a pleasure to be asked to write books for both you and The Shadows.

I've really appreciated your support of my musicals and crikey…you've even been there in times of romantic turbulence! What a pal.

I was pleased to be there at your 40th, playing with my band at your 50th and being part of the unforgettable Mediterranean cruise for the 60th.

It was always a pleasure, to support The Tennis Foundation helping to raise money for young tennis players, be it at Brighton, Birmingham, Hampton Court or even in the depths

of the Australian jungle!

As I see it, you've made some of the best records of the last 50 years, been true to yourself, your beliefs, your friends and your music as well as being a great ambassador abroad.

We've been so lucky to be a part of such a unique musical era.

Keep on Rockin',

Mike Read

1940–1950

Harry Rodger Webb was born in Lucknow, India on October 14th 1940 to Rodger and Dorothy Webb and his eldest sister Donella was born three years later.

The young Harry started school in 1945, at an establishment attached to St. Thomas' Church in Lucknow and where he first sang in the choir.

Cliff's second sister, Jacqueline was born in 1948, the year that the family made the three-week voyage to England on the SS Ranghi which landed them at Tilbury Docks.

The Webb's arrived in Britain in September 1948, with just £5 to their name, the equivalent of a week's wages (now about £400.) The family moved into a single room in Carshalton, Surrey at a time when a quarter of British homes still had no electricity, there were only 15,000 TV sets in the whole country and most families relied on the radio for their entertainment. The long-running radio serial Mrs. Dales Diary had just started and one of the most popular radio shows was It's That Man Again (ITMA) starring Tommy Handley, Dereyck Guyler and Hattie Jacques. Popular songs in the UK at the time included Buttons and Bows, Baby Face, Red Roses For A Blue Lady, Slow Boat To China and I'm Looking Over A Four-Leaf Clover.

The young Harry was enrolled at Stanley Park Road Primary School in Carshalton, but for much of the following year his father, Rodger was unable to find work and the family struggled to make ends meet.

It didn't stop their son from finding his first girlfriend in school pal, Elizabeth Sayers.

1950-1960

Post-war jobs for unskilled workers were mainly available in factories, so the Webb's moved to Waltham Cross in Hertfordshire where Rodger got a job with Ferguson's Radio at Enfield and Dorothy found work at a factory in Broxbourne, after giving birth to their last child, Joan.

It was a new school for young Harry as he started at King's Road Primary at Waltham Cross.

In 1952 Harry failed the 11 plus exam and went to Cheshunt Secondary Modern School and the following year was selected for both the school and Hertfordshire Under 14s football teams in what was known then as 'right-back.' The family moved into a three-bedroom council house in Hargreaves Close, Cheshunt.

His first-ever public appearance as a singer was at a Youth fellowship dance in Cheshunt, which led, in the mid-50s to Harry becoming involved in the school dramatic society, being cast as Ratty in Wind In The Willows and Bob Cratchit in Charles Dickens' A Christmas Carol. Two teachers at the school who influenced him enormously were Mr. Norris and Bill Latham.

In 1957 Harry is stripped of his prefect's badge for playing truant from school to watch Bill Haley and the Comets at Edmonton on March 3rd. Their current single was Don't Knock The Rock.

Harry left Cheshunt Secondary Modern with an O Level in English and began work as a credit control clerk at Atlas Lamps in Enfield for £4-15-0d a week. Outside working hours he was singing with musical group The Quintones alongside school-friends Beryl Molyneux, Freda Johnson, John Vince and Betty Clark, the group performing at the local Holy Trinity Church Youth Club.

During 1958, drummer Terry Smart co-opted Harry into the Dick Teague Skiffle Group as vocalist and rhythm guitarist, but Terry and Harry soon took their leave to form The Drifters, enlisting a former school-friend of Harry's, guitarist Norman Mitham.

Playing more Rock & Roll based music, they rehearsed at the Webb's house and after a gig at The Five Horseshoes in Hoddesdon, 18-year-old teddy boy John Foster was so impressed with Harry's singing that he offered to be their manager. Under his management they extended their

gigs, but at one show in Derby the promoter let it be known that he didn't consider Harry Webb & The Drifters to be a very commercial name and suggested that Harry, at least, should change his name. After initial suggestions of Cliff Russard and Russ Clifford the name Cliff Richard was decided upon and after a gig at London's 2i's coffee bar bass player Ian Samwell joined the group.

In the early summer of 1958 John Foster's parents put up £10 to enable Cliff and The Drifters to make a demonstration record of Lloyd Price's Lawdy Miss Clawdy and Jerry Lee Lewis' Breathless at the HMV Studios in London's Oxford Street. The Drifters line-up that recorded these demos was Cliff, Ian Samwell, Norman Mitham, Terry Smart and Ken Pavey.

Cliff and The Drifters were the star attraction at a Carrol Levis Discovery talent show at The Gaumont Theatre, Shepherd's Bush. They cleverly offered to top the bill without having to take part in the contest a masterstroke that led to agent George Ganjou agreeing to sign them to his agency.

After hearing their demonstration record and being impressed, producer Norrie Paramor agreed to take Cliff and The Drifters into Abbey Road Studios in July, where they laid down Schoolboy Crush and a song written by Ian Samwell, Move It, following which he signed a long-term contract with EMI's Columbia label. After the recording the group undertook a nine-week residency at Butlin's holiday camp in Clacton-on-Sea, with Ken Pavey replacing Norman Mitham.

Schoolboy Crush was scheduled to be the A side of the first release, but Norrie Paramor's daughter told her father that Move It would have far more appeal to teenagers, so on September 12th Move It entered the chart with Cliff making his debut on ABC TV's Oh Boy, the following day singing Move It and Don't Bug Me Baby.

As the record moved up the chart, Cliff and The Drifters were booked to appear on a nationwide tour with The Kalin Twins, Hal and Herbie and the Most Brothers, Mickie Most and Alex Murray. John Foster went to the 2i's coffee bar to try and recruit guitarist Tony Sheridon for the tour, but he was at the cinema and Hank Marvin, formerly with Newcastle's Railroaders Skiffle Group and Pete Chester's Chesternuts was recommended to him.

Hank agreed, but only if fellow Railroader and Chesternut, Bruce Welch could come in on rhythm guitar. The Drifters line-up on tour was Hank, Bruce, Terry Smart and Ian Samwell, with Most Brothers bass guitarist Jet Harris also playing for them on the tour, after which he replaced Samwell full-time.t

Realising the need for professional management, the experienced Franklin Boyd came on board, with John Foster still working as part of the team.

Following his radio debut on the BBC's Saturday Club, Columbia released Cliff's second single, High Class Baby, which peaked at No 7 and established him as a new artist for whom a bright future is predicted. After just two hit singles, he landed the part of Curly Thompson in the film Serious Charge, alongside Anthony Quayle, Sarah Churchill and Andrew Ray.

1959

Cliff later commented on his role in the film Serious Charge; 'The people who made the film must have been daft. I was cast as Curly, but instead of simply changing the name of the character, they went the painful and complicated procedure of curling my hair with hot tongs every morning before the day's shooting!'

Early in 1959, both Franklin Boyd and John Foster were dismissed, as Tito Burns became Cliff's new manager at the time of the third single, Livin' Lovin' Doll. Although the single only reached No 20, it's noteworthy, as it's the first time that Hank, Bruce and Jet have played on one of Cliff's singles.

Move It was voted Best New Single in the NME as drummer Terry Smart left to join the Merchant Navy and was replaced by a drummer suggested by Jet Harris, Tony Meehan, who had formerly played behind Adam Faith, Vince Taylor and Vince Eager. Tony joined just in time to play on Cliff's first album, a live studio session at Abbey Road and on a session that yielded Dynamite and Never Mind, the latter being released as a double A side with Mean Streak.

Part of Cliff's deal with his role in Serious Charge was that a single had to be released, but both he and The Drifters weren't keen on the up tempo rock & roll track Living Doll. Bruce Welch suggested a much slower, almost country tempo that transformed the song to such an extent that it topped the chart and became a million seller, winning Cliff his first Gold Disc. With the emergence of Cliff as a major star, the American Drifters insisted on a name change for Cliff's group, Jet Harris suggested the name that would be enthusiastically adopted: The Shadows.

Only a year after the paper had referred to him as 'a crude exhibitionist,' the New Musical Express described Cliff as 'The most electrifying and dynamic vocal talent to emerge in recent years,' and included a four-page tribute. Cliff commented, 'One short year and yet I seem to have accomplished so much…I've been very lucky. Without the public there would be no Cliff Richard success story…I shall never forget what they've done for me. In spite of all the insults hurled at today's teenagers, I think they're a great crowd. I should know after all, I'm one of them.' He also admitted, 'Marriage is my ultimate aim…but not until I'm 27.'

Cliff's second film Expresso Bongo was released in the Autumn of 1959, in which he starred alongside Laurence Harvey, Sylvia Syms and Yolande Donlan in his role as 'Bongo Herbert.'

Despite this being his second film in the short 12 months he'd been on the scene, he was confident to declare, 'My ultimate ambition is to make a western with Elvis.'

The dubious comments of the critics following the premiere of Expresso Bongo included, 'Not enough numbers,' 'Not enough professionalism,' and 'No colour.' Compensation came in the form of being voted 'King of Rock & Roll' on Radio Luxembourg's Swoon Club, 'Best British Male Vocalist of the Year' on TV's Cool For Cats and appearing in pantomime, with The Shadows, in Babes In The Wood.

As Travellin' Light climbed the UK chart, Living Doll entered the lower reaches of the US chart and Bruce Forsyth presented Cliff with a Gold Disc for Living Doll during his debut on the top-rated show Sunday Night At The London Palladium.

1960

*"Every time he takes a microphone
in his hand
They scream and they shout
And they know just what it's all
about
Cos there ain't another boy who
can move it around like Cliff."*

*They Call Him Cliff – Don Lang,
1960*

The final year of the 50s had been exceptional for Cliff, but would be surpassed by the first two years of the 60s, with all of his nine singles reaching the top four and two making it to No 1.

Early in 1960 Cliff and the boys undertook their first US tour, alongside Freddy Cannon, Frankie Avalon, Johnny & the Hurricanes, Clyde McPhatter, Sammy Turner and The Clovers. The 38 dates included Pittsburgh, San Antonio, Kansas City, Milwaukee, Oklahoma City, Dallas, Indianapolis, Houston and Buddy Holly's hometown, Lubbock.

During the Stateside trip Cliff appeared on Pat Boone's TV Show, with the host introducing him as 'Britain's most important singing and record star.' And ending the show with the comment, 'Cliff should have a long and impressive show business career.' Spot on Pat.

With The Shadows remaining in the States to fulfil tour commitments, Cliff flew back from Kansas City to appear at the NME Poll Winner's Concert and was supported by a group of his choice, The Parker Royal Four.

Influential TV producer Jack Good expressed his thoughts that Cliff would echo many times down the years, 'I don't think Cliff Richard would have existed at all as a singer without Elvis. He certainly wouldn't be the singer he is today. The initial impetus of Cliff's singing was entirely due to Elvis Presley's influence.' Fellow singer Marty Wilde agreed, 'Without Elvis Presley the main influence of Rock & Roll would never have appeared, so neither would Cliff Richard. Lionel Bart, the writer of Living Doll, concurred, 'I must concede that Jack Good is being perfectly reasonable when he states that Cliff was considerably influenced by Elvis,'

Cliff himself had the last word, 'I feel that without Elvis I certainly wouldn't be the singer I am today. I'd like to go on record as saying that in my opinion Elvis Presley is the greatest,' while in an interview with Elvis himself, prior to him leaving the army, he admits to having Cliff's records in his collection.

On the same time that Expresso Bongo opened in New York, Cliff recorded a B side, five songs for the Me & My Shadows album and two songs that became hit singles, Nine Times Out Of Ten and Gee Whiz It's You. The latter song they had started to write on a plane, after a stewardess asked how they went about writing a song.

In between recording, Cliff had a tight schedule that took in TV shows such as Crackerjack, Sunday Night At The London Palladium, ATV's Sunday Spectacular, ATV's Me & My Shadows, The Royal Variety Show as well as a tour of the UK, starring at the Royal Albert Hall, and a long run at the London Palladium on a show which included Des O'Connor and Russ Conway.

On the subject of The Royal Variety Show, Cliff commented,

'…I'm completely knocked out to be selected again! In fact everything is going so well at the moment I'm scared to breathe in case something goes wrong. Nervous? Of course I am. My stomach is turning seventy-five cartwheels every minute…'

In just 18 months he'd had eight hit singles, become Britain's most popular singer and now, in 1960, was mingling with Prince Philip, the Duchess of Kent, Princess Alexandra and performing for the Queen and the Queen Mother. He celebrated modestly by moving into a semi-detached house in Winchmore Hill with his parents and three sisters and bought a grey Sunbeam Alpine sports car.

In an unprecedented move, Cliff's record label threw a party for 80 teenagers to help them decide which of the 24 songs of Cliff's should be his ninth single. The youngsters, drawn from Cliff's fan club, EMI staff and various youth organisations gave the most votes to Please Don't Tease, followed by Gee Whiz It's You and Nine Times Out Of Ten.

Cliff and The Shadows also landed their own show on Radio Luxembourg, called, appropriately enough, Me & My Shadows, and opened each programme with their version of the 1927 classic of the same name made famous by Al Jolson. The series began in the summer of 1960, with each show running for 15 minutes and often featured classics like My Babe, What'd I Say, See You In My Dreams and I Got A Woman as well as songs from the Me & My Shadows album. When the album was released, music paper headlines boldly proclaimed, 'No home should be without this album by Cliff.' They were right; it remains one of the finest albums of the period and is thought by many fans to be Cliff and The Shadows' greatest album.

The icing on the cake in 1960 was being voted Best British Singer, runner-up to Elvis Presley as World Male Singer with The Shadows' Apache and Please Don't Tease being voted first and second Best British Disc of the Year.

1961

At the beginning of 1961 it was revealed that Cliff had spent more weeks on the chart in the previous 12 months than any other artist, beating Adam Faith, Elvis Presley and The Everly Brothers.

The year got off to a flying start with Cliff's own series on ATV, an appearance at the Royal Albert Hall and a tour with Norman Vaughan, Chas McDevitt and Shirley Douglas and Dave Sampson & the Hunters.

It was not only the British fans who were buying Cliff's records as his records charted around the world, with India having no less than five of his songs in their top 10 in February 1961. In March, Cliff and The Shadows set off for a lengthy tour, taking in Australia, New Zealand, Singapore, Malaya and South Africa. Well, they actually started by going to see a horror film in Hounslow first, as there was a lengthy delay at London Airport! When the globetrotting Cliff returned to the UK, he commented, 'The only minor upset of the tour was the controversy over the colour bar, which prevented some of the non-Europeans from seeing our show. When we were first offered the contract to go to South Africa we didn't realise there would be those problems and when they arose we found ourselves in rather an awkward position. We overcame this situation to the best of our ability by offering to do a couple of shows for the non-Europeans with the proceeds going to charity.'

At the time of Cliff's 12th single, Theme For A Dream,(with advance orders of over 200,000) a new film was discussed, as yet untitled, but his agent Tito Burns revealed that Cliff could make as much as £30,000 from it.

In the early part of the year, Cliff appeared on programmes such as Teen Beat, Parade of the Pops a London Palladium Special for the USA, and Crackerjack, as the music press asked whether The Shadows, now very successful in their own right, should split from Cliff. Australian Peter Gormley, who had already been looking after The Shadows, became Cliff's new manager in a move which brought a long period of stability to his career. There was no contract, just a gentleman's agreement that if it wasn't working from either side then either of them could walk away. Neither of them ever walked away.

In the spring, Cliff made his debut on Juke Box Jury alongside Dora Bryan, Janet Munro and DJ Ray Orchard, before heading off on a UK tour of one-night stands interspersed with appearances on Saturday Club, Parade

of the Pops and with fans having the chance to buy the 'Cliff Richard two-way shirt' in black & white for just 32/6d.

In the same month that his father died aged just 57, Cliff's new film The Young Ones was announced. He coped with the grief, whilst embracing another big screen challenge: 'It's not often that I get nervous, but boy those butterflies really got at me for the whole of the first day's shooting and stayed with me for almost the rest of the week.' Of his co-stars he said, 'I have benefited enormously as a result of working with such a fine actor as Robert Morley and I've been getting along wonderfully with Carole (Gray), she's a great girl and everyone likes her.'

In the early summer, Cliff's 14th single, A Girl Like you was released and he appeared on The Billy Cotton Band Show, Saturday Club, Radio Luxembourg Spectacular, and the Jo Stafford Show for the United States.

While doing a Blackpool season with The Shadows, impresario Leslie Grade took Cliff to watch Preston North End play Leyton Orient, who were in the old First Division that season; the only time in their history.

Far Right: Poster
for the musical
The Young Ones,
released in 1961.

A couple of months later they went to watch Leyton Orient play Norwich City, which was not that much of a surprise as Cliff had once played football for Hertfordshire Juniors.

In the month of his 21st birthday, Cliff released his 15th single When The Girl In Your Arms Is The Girl In Your Heart, which he performed on TV's Thank Your Lucky Stars. Hank Marvin commented, 'Cliff has been the perfect ambassador for British show business wherever he has travelled' and Bruce Welch added, 'Despite all the success that has come his way, he hasn't become the slightest bit big-headed. Shadows drummer Tony Meehan said, 'He is undoubtedly one of the finest people character-wise with whom I have ever come into contact. He has great quality and patience and is a wonderful example to all the young people who admire him.'

As Cliff played Australia and New Zealand in the autumn of 1961, it was announced that his new film would be called Summer Holiday and that once again he had been voted Best British Male Singer and was second to Elvis in the World Male Singer category.

From the other side of the world he wrote a 'Dear John' letter to a girl he'd been seeing fairly regularly, Delia Wicks.

He said it was 'one of the biggest decisions' he would ever have to make, before urging her to 'find someone who is free to love you as you deserve to be loved' and who 'is able to marry you'. He continued: 'I couldn't give up my career, besides the fact that my mother and sisters, since my father's death, rely on me completely. I have showbiz in my blood now and I would be lost without it.' Delia – who performed in the then-popular Black and White Minstrel Show – was said to have been heartbroken by Cliff's decision to break off the romance. The Young Ones was heralded by the critics as 'The best musical Britain has ever made…and the finest teenage screen entertainment produced for a long time…anywhere!'

At the end of 1961 Tony Meehan left The Shadows to be replaced by former member of Marty Wilde's wildcats Brain Bennett. The last well-known track that Tony played on was Do You Want To Dance and Brian's were Dancing Shoes and Summer Holiday, having written the latter song with Bruce Welch.

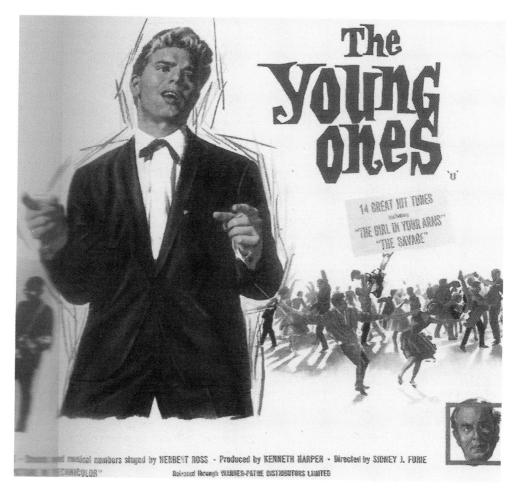

1962

Cliff's 16th single, The Young Ones was released at the beginning of January 1962 and became only the fourth single in the history of the UK chart to perform the feat. One of those was the first-ever No 1 on the first-ever chart and the other two were Elvis singles, so no mean achievement.

With a fifth chart-topping single to his name, the Variety Club of Great Britain presented him with the 'Show Business Personality of the Year' award and he sang in front of Princess Margaret and Lord Snowdon, joining them afterwards for tea and cakes. Cliff and Lord Snowdon discussed their cars, a black Cadillac and a Mini-Cooper respectively, the singer reporting that

the couple were 'Marvellously friendly people.'

A special copy of the film The Young Ones was later sent to the Princess at Clarence House.

In April, Cliff and The Shadows headlined the NME Poll Winners Concert at Wembley, which turned out to be the last performance with the group by Jet Harris, who would be replaced by Brian 'Licorice' Locking who'd played bass with Marty Wilde.

In the NME 10th anniversary book, pianist Russ Conway revealed Cliff's sense of humour, which had included completely filling his dressing room from floor to ceiling with hundreds of balloons and filling someone else's dressing room with dozens of pieces of junk, seemingly from well-wishers.

Whilst performing his 17th single, I'm Looking Out The Window on Thank Your Lucky Stars, Cliff was presented with a Gold Disc for The Young Ones by DJ Pete Murray who also presented The Shadows with a Gold Disc for Apache.

May saw Charlie Chaplin's daughter Geraldine being screen-tested for the part of Cliff's girlfriend in Summer Holiday, Cliff back at Leyton Orient, but singing this time instead of cheering, Cliff and The Shadows flying to Paris to watch Ray Charles and the start of rehearsals for the new film.

Summer Holiday began to take shape at a gymnasium in Paddington with the girl who did get the part as Cliff's girlfriend, Laurie Peters on board.

The double-decker bus trip across Europe to Greece has now become part of British folk-lore, but Cliff did actually have to learn to drive the vehicle. He said at the time, 'I found it unexpectedly easy really; the only thing that fooled me was the length which I found difficult to manage. Three double-decker buses are already in Europe waiting for us…there's only one bus actually featured in the film, but rather than cart it all around the Continent we've got three dotted about in various places and we shall use them when we come to them.'

In the summer of 1962, reminiscing on his four years at the top he admitted, 'Sometimes I think my mother will wake me up one morning and I'll find myself back to being just plain Harry Rodger Webb, an ordinary clerk. I mean I'm 22 years old now and when I realise that I can't even remember my fourteenth birthday it gets pretty frightening.'

His singles continue to chart around the world as a re-working of Jerry Lee Lewis' It'll Be Me, becomes his 18th UK single.

October saw the release of It's Wonderful To Be Young (US title) in America, giving Cliff the chance to meet Elvis' father Vernon, visit Graceland and also meet Nat King Cole, Bobby Darin and Paul Anka.

Then it was back to England for another Royal Variety Show, more accolades including being voted Best British Male Singer yet again and promoting his 19th single, The Next Time and Bachelor Boy.

1963

The Next Time/Bachelor Boy became the first No 1 of the New Year and stayed on top until being deposed by The Shadows' Dance On. Despite the onslaught of The Beatles and an enormous sea-change on the British music scene, Cliff and The Shadows were destined to have one of their best-ever years. Singles were now 6/3d and LPs 30/11d and in 1963 the outfit that began back in 1959 would shift millions of them.

Mid-January saw Cliff and The Shadows touring South Africa, as Summer Holiday had been premiered in London and South Africa simultaneously.

On apartheid he said, 'I agree that I'm not qualified to talk about it, but we did not go to Africa to delve into the racial question. We went there to entertain and perform, but if writers persist in asking me about it I have to make some comment…even if it's only to brush it aside because it's not my territory.'

The papers became aware of Cliff's relationship with dancer Jackie Irving and they also compared his new film favourably, one critic claiming Summer Holiday had far more 'freshness and zest than Girls, Girls, Girls, Elvis' new movie.

Cliff's 20th single, the title track from Summer Holiday, was a shoe-in for the No 1 spot and February saw four titles from the film in the top 30, the first artist to achieve such a feat. No wonder he bought his mother a new Chevrolet, was driving a Cadillac himself and had ordered a Thunderbird!

The songs from the film were also riding high in Israel, France, Norway, South Africa, Holland, Sweden and Hong Kong.

When it was estimated that he would earn £6,000 for co-writing Bachelor Boy with Bruce Welch, Cliff said 'I've always enjoyed writing, but I've never really considered myself a great composer...normally I throw my number together very quickly. I get fed up with them after a while. I'm afraid I'm not like Bruce Welch, he can churn 'em out by the dozen.'

At Bruce's birthday, in April, Cliff and The Shadows were joined by The Beatles as they parodied each others hits, Cliff commenting that The Beatles were, 'The greatest bunch of boys I've met since The Shadows.'

As Cliff's fame increased, the press were even quoting his tailor, Dougie Millings, 'I've been making Cliff's suits since he appeared at the 2i's coffee bar, which is practically underneath my premises. Cliff, in fact, was the first big name I ever made suits for. He's got a very good figure from a tailor's point of view... regular measurements and no faults to cover up. If Cliff needs a suit for stage work, then the most popular is Italian silk, but it's a bit expensive... about £40.'

The spring saw the release of Cliff's new single, Lucky Lips, his own TV spectacular being screened and a lengthy recording session with The Shadows, in Spain.

The summer brought another season at Blackpool, the publication of Life With Cliff Richard for just 3/6d, another party with The Beatles and the announcement of the next film, Wonderful Life.

An avid film fan, Cliff revealed that among his favourites were, Guys & Dolls, Calamity Jane, The Magnificent Seven, Shane, and High Noon but his No 1 was West Side Story, 'I think it is the best film ever made...it has everything, a great story, fabulous songs and dancing that's out of this world.'

Despite some claims that it sounded too much like an old Elvis song, Lucky Lips topped the chart in Norway, Sweden, Hong Kong, South Africa, Holland and Israel, as well as giving Cliff his first US hit since Living Doll. This prompted US composer Roy Bennett, who with his partner Sid Tepper, had written several successful songs for Cliff including The Young Ones, Travellin' Light, When The Girl In Your Arms and 'D' In Love, to fly to London to pitch new songs to the singer, although he wouldn't actually meet him for another 40 years! 'We'd be delighted if he'd consider using more songs by us, remembering that he has featured our songs in the past.'

At the time of his fifth anniversary in the business, Cliff talked about how he saw the next five years. 'I think things will slow down tremendously. Success is all very well, but it becomes pointless if one is unable to secure and solidify that position. My great ambition is to play Heathcliff in Wuthering Heights.'

On being asked about marriage,

he replied, 'I have always thought I would marry at 27 simply because I regard it as the most suitable age for a man to marry. However the situation doesn't arise at the moment because there are no prospects in view.'

The press continued to link him with dancer Jackie Irving, to which Cliff responded, 'It's true that I've taken Jackie out more than any other girl, but then being placed as I am, it's only natural that I should take out girls I know rather than those I don't know.'

As his 22nd single, It's All In The Game was released, Cliff was asked to name his top 10 favourite records, he included Bill Haley's Rock Around The Clock, The Shadows' FBI, Ray Charles' Drown In My Own Tears and Elvis Presley's Heartbreak Hotel.

In the autumn, a two-week tour of Israel is followed by an appearance on the Ed Sullivan Show in the States, a tour of France and the announcement that Cliff's new film Wonderful Life will be shot in The Canaries with Susan Hampshire co-starring.

Cliff promoted his 23rd single, Don't Talk To Him, another collaboration with Bruce Welch, on Thank Your Lucky Stars, Sunday Night At The London Palladium, Parade of the Pops and The Royal Variety Show.

In November, Cliff commented on the fact that his £30,000 six-bedroom Tudor-style home in Upper Nazeing, had been discovered by fans, resulting in the national papers carrying a story about a guard with dogs and a gun. 'That's a lot of rubbish, especially about the Alsatians. We've only got a poodle! It was my chauffeur's way of being funny, but on that day he had a bad scriptwriter.'

Cliff was ecstatic as he not only won the title of Best British Male Singer in the NME poll, but for the first time beat Elvis in the World Male Singer section. He reckoned that in all the excitement over The Beatles that they'd momentarily forgotten about Elvis and he'd been able to sneak in and clinch the title.

On Christmas Day, The Shadows' new bass player John Rostill makes his debut with the group, as Cliff and The Shadows star in a pre-recorded hour-long TV spectacular.

Far Left: 10th January 1963: Cliff fiddles with his ring during a tele-recorded BBC interview.

1964

At the beginning of the year Cliff talked about his fellow artists…

Elvis: Around the World thousands copied him. Some simply grew Elvis sideburns, some styled their hair the Presley way and others sold their bicycles and put down a deposit on a guitar.

Frank Sinatra: I spent an afternoon with him at Northwood, Middlesex when he visited the British blind children. They flocked around him feeling for his hands. 'Oi, Sinarcher,' cried one blind Cockney boy of six, 'Come 'an see the sandpit.'

Adam Faith: Even a six–figure win on the pools wouldn't give you the satisfaction, adventure and thrill of living that has come the way of Adam and me.

Billy Fury: Off-stage he doesn't strike me as furious at all. He talks quietly and laughs quietly…on stage it's different.

In a survey by Billboard Magazine, using the sales charts of 34 countries outside America, Cliff emerged as world champion, with Elvis second and The Shadows third. Such accolades didn't give him delusions of grandeur, which was demonstrated in a New Year interview that same month.

'I hope for a year of peace and prosperity for all mankind, and for the betterment of International relations and understanding. If in some small way The Shadows and I can help the spread of British goodwill abroad, then I shall be very happy.'

The new film Wonderful Life was shot in The Canaries early in the year, but dogged by bad weather and having to ride camels. The camels didn't come easy to Cliff: 'Don't imagine it's like riding a horse; that would be fatal. What you have to do is watch his droopy eyes, get ready for grunts and then hang on like grim death, because it's rougher than a roller-coaster ride!'

While he was filming, his 24th single, I'm The Lonely One was released and he arranged to buy a house in Albufeira on the coast of Portugal.

In March and April there was a three-week UK tour, a gold disc for Lucky Lips, the release of the 25th single, Constantly and the NME Poll Winners Concert. It was also revealed that agent Leslie Grade had turned down offers for Cliff to appear in Las Vegas and Beirut, although rumours abounded about a Hollywood musical and a Hollywood movie.

Far Right: Cliff at home with his mother and sisters.

Later in the spring came a tour in France, Belgium, Holland and Germany, with The Shadows, for which Cliff, at various times, had to sing in four languages.

Despite all his success, at the time of the release of the 26th single, On The Beach, Cliff confessed that he wasn't as well-off as folk might imagine: 'People think I must be a millionaire. I'm not. Nowhere near it. I have to ask my accountant if I can afford it before making any really big purchase.'

Wonderful Life was released in 40 different cities with the London premiere being attended by Princess Alexandra and her husband Angus Ogilvy, with the proceeds of the evening going to the National Association of Youth Clubs. One film critic wrote, 'He (Cliff) improves with every picture he makes. Not only is his acting much more convincing, but he also displays considerable talent as a light comedian and impressionist.'

During the summer, Cliff recorded in Nashville and New York, but admitted that he'd also love to record in Chicago. 'That's the home of the great writer Curtis Mayfield and that superb group The Impressions. Nothing would make me happier than to record a Mayfield song with The Impressions backing me!'

At the time of the release of the 27th single, The Twelfth of Never, it was announced that advance orders for his forthcoming three and a half month run at the London Palladium in Aladdin, with The Shadows, Una Stubbs and Arthur Askey were the highest in the theatre's history.

Just after another Royal Variety show, the 28th single was released hard on the heels of The Twelfth of Never, and I Could Easily Fall was featured in

Aladdin. It was also announced that a screen version would be made, complete with enormous budget and a re-written storyline.

In the end of year NME poll, Cliff was voted Best British Male Singer and Best British Vocal Personality.

1965

In the New Year Cliff revealed his hopes and plans for 1965. 'I trust that my next film is well liked. It won't be a musical really, you see, as there are only about four songs in it. I don't think I want to undertake any tours this year. The panto season doesn't finish until May 10th and we start filming soon after that.'

The private companies of Cliff and Frank Ifield were taken over by Constellation Investments, bringing them £474,000, the Daily Express commenting: 'Most of the money concerned is likely to go to Cliff Richard, which will almost certainly establish him as a millionaire.'

By May the company was doing so well on the Stock Exchange that Cliff and Frank's shares were worth £730,000.

In an interview on the subject of earnings Cliff commented: 'I leave it to the businessmen. All I've asked is that they tell me six months before I go broke so that I can get out.'

The press also suggested that he was about to retire to live in Portugal.

'The truth is that sooner or later I do hope to retire from the business. Let's face it that's the ultimate ambition of most entertainers. We can't go on forever and the time must come when we have to quit. I would rather leave while I am at the top than wait for the public to turn its back on me.'

With I Could Easily Fall and The Twelfth of Never still in various charts around the world, Cliff's 29th single The Minute You're Gone was released in the early spring. Seven weeks later, the song, recorded in Nashville, knocked Unit Four Plus Two's Concrete & Clay off the No 1 spot.

This was followed by another single recorded in the US, On My Word, a short tour of Scandinavia and a tour of Spain, France and Switzerland.

In an interview with Disc magazine, Cliff discussed his eating habits.

'I never eat lunch, apart from something like cheese and biscuits. I don't even have breakfast or a good meal when I get home in the evening...I've got to look after my weight.' He was also, as always asked about marriage again. 'I would like to get married very much eventually...I've no-one in particular in mind at present. There have been a couple of false alarms which I wouldn't like to happen again.'

Above: Wearing a dressing gown Cliff enjoys a cup of coffee in the kitchen.

August brought news of the next film, due to go into production in November, with manager Peter Gormley insisting that it's 'altogether more sophisticated than his last pictures.'

Cliff's 31st single was also released in August. The Time In Between saw him reunited in record with The Shadows, after two US singles. Shadows' Hank Marvin commented, 'We were thinking of cutting The Time In Between, but when Cliff heard it he was so enthusiastic about it we passed it over to him.'

In October, Cliff and The Shadows flew across the Iron Curtain to play dates in Warsaw, before performing in Beirut and the French Film Industry's Gala Concert in Paris in the presence of Princess Grace of Monaco.

This was followed by a series of one-nighters in France, at the time that Cliff was declared Israel's most popular artist and the BBC presented the biographical radio documentary The Cliff Richard Story.

In the autumn of 1965, there were mediocre reviews for Cliff's 32nd single, another song recorded in Nashville, Wind Me Up, but despite the critics it provided Cliff with another hit. 'It just shows that you have to take adverse criticism with a pinch of salt. Frankly, I've given up worrying…it's impossible to please everyone all the time. Actually it was Bruce Welch's brainwave to release Wind Me Up, and it was his suggestion that we released It's All In The Game and The Twelfth Of Never.

Towards the end of the year there was still some confusion over the next film, which Cliff attempted to clarify. 'The last news to be announced was that we would make this film together and start work on the screen adaptation of Aladdin some time in 1966. Now all that has changed and Aladdin is definitely going to be the next film.'

From late November Cliff and the Shadows undertook a UK tour of one-night stands after which came the NME poll and Cliff yet again won Best British Male Singer and came second to Elvis in the World category. 'I regard myself as a very fortunate person, for this is the eighth time you have bestowed poll honours on me…I want you to know that I value it deeply.'

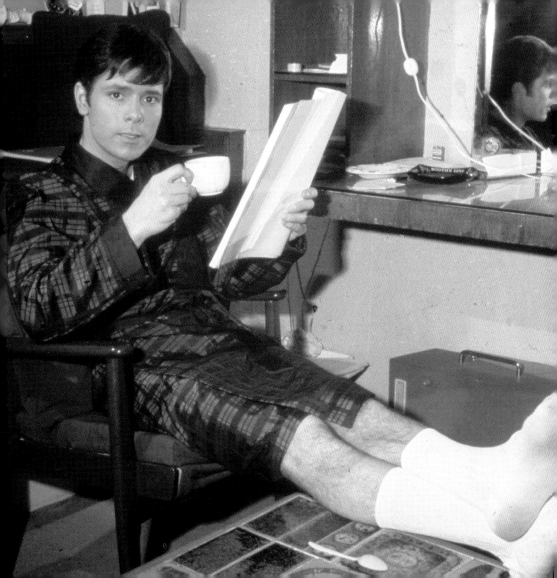

1966

Far Right: Cliff
has some fun with
Vivienne Ventura,
during a break
in shooting his
new film 'Finders
Keepers' at
Pinewood Studios.

Cliff surprised many by releasing Blue Turns To Grey as his first single of 1966, a song written by Rolling Stones' Mick Jagger and Keith Richards. As the film version of Aladdin now looked less likely to come to fruition, Cliff appeared on such programmes as Pop Inn and Thank Your Lucky Stars promoting the new single. At the invitation of the Bishop of Coventry, he also took part in a service at the Royal Albert Hall to mark the 25th anniversary of the Abbey Christian Community and announced that he would be spending two weeks camping in Cornwall with the Crusader Union. Questioned about his increasing amount of Christian activities Cliff replied: 'It's perfectly true that I would like to take up teaching at some time in the future. After all I have to be sensible and think ahead, because I can't expect to remain a star for the rest of my life.'

In April, it was announced that Cliff would play Buttons in the London Palladium production of Cinderella, he and The Shadows featured in ABC's 10th anniversary programme and they appeared at The NME Poll Winners Concert alongside The Beatles, the Rolling Stones and Roy Orbison.

The following month, production started at Pinewood Studios on Finders Keepers, Cliff's fifth film and featured The Shadows, Peggy Mount, Robert Morley, Graham Stark and the 20-year-old alleged girlfriend of Marlon Brando, Vivien Ventura.

She commented, 'Cliff's so happy he makes me happy. When we have a romantic scene we go into a corner to work things out. He is so open to suggestions and has so many good ideas himself that it's a joy to be in a picture with him…I'm a lucky girl.'

The early summer saw Cliff appearing on the 400th edition of BBC's Saturday Club and a couple of weeks later he took the stage at a Billy Graham Crusade meeting at London's Earls Court to sing It's No Secret and announced to the audience of 25,000 that he was a Christian. He also declared his intention to embark on a three-year divinity course when his pantomime finished in April 1967. The press were keen to know more.

'Someone suggested it was sissy

to proclaim your Christian beliefs, but I don't think it is. I feel great all the time and I know it is because of my beliefs. I've felt this way for two years now and it has relieved me of the petty jealousy one gets in show business and helped me to help others…'

In July Cliff sold his house in Essex for £43,500. The 34th single, Visions was released and Cliff was still talking of his desire to play Heathcliff in Wuthering Heights.

In the autumn he was talking even more expansively about his convictions: 'My whole life has been changed because of a healthier state of mind. I believe there is only one way to live and that's by the Bible. It's the only source that is completely reliable, and I set my own life on this. If you've got a focal point in your life you can't fail. The Church has been the biggest influence in my life…'

In October, the 35th single Time Drags By was released, the song immediately being raved about by Paul McCartney. Cliff performed it while topping the bill on the TV show Sunday Night At The London Palladium, after which he was presented with a 10,000-strong petition begging him not to leave show business. The same month, Cliff joined the Archbishop of York and the Bishop of Coventry on stage at the Royal Albert Hall, saying, 'As a Christian I feel it is my duty to take every opportunity to profess I am a Christian and that I personally was saved by Jesus Christ.'

Later that month he appeared with tow clergymen at a Christian meeting in Liverpool, saying: 'People do not realise how easy it is to become a Christian… and I hope that whether you are Christians or not, your ears have been opened to Christianity.'

The Sunday Express reported that Cliff was to be confirmed as a member of the Church of England.

The year ended with the release of the film Thunderbirds Are Go, which incorporated puppet replicas of Cliff and The Shadows and featured them on four numbers.

Left: 28th November 1966: Cliff at a rehearsal for ITV's Royal Gala Show.

1967

While many in the industry were heading towards flower power, the summer of love and blowing their minds, Cliff burst on the scene in 1967 with an outspoken interview: 'I'm not being self-righteous, I just want to get out of this business because I feel I have to. When I leave depends on the result of my religious O level examination. Don't think I regard everybody in show business as sinful; I love the atmosphere and the life. If I didn't want to teach Religious Instruction in a secondary school, I'd stay in it till Doomsday. When I give up this life it's not going to be a complete break; I don't think people realise that I'll still be making records. I just want to be an ordinary teacher in an ordinary secondary school.'

In March, having been voted the best-dressed male star, his 37th single, It's All Over, written by Don Everly was released.

Rumours abounded that Cliff and The Shadows were to go their separate ways, but the gossip was quickly stopped by their manager:

'The misunderstanding has arisen because The Shadows are touring abroad while Cliff is making a religious film which starts shooting in June and continues into July. They will get together again in

September to work on the dramatic film inspired by the Vietnam War.'

During April and May Cliff recorded many religious songs for the album Good News, including When I Survey The Wondrous Cross, What A Friend We Have In Jesus, Take My Hand Precious Lord and the 23rd Psalm.

He took time off from recording to appear on the 450th anniversary of the BBC's radio series Saturday Club, the NME Poll Winners Concert, Juke Box Jury and to promote his 38th single, Neil Diamond's I'll Come Runnin' which was released at the beginning of June.

The summer saw Cliff filming Two A Penny, a movie with a £150,000 budget, for evangelist Billy Graham, with all the proceeds going to charity. The actors' union Equity refused to allow Cliff to appear in the film for nothing and insisted on a payment of £40 a week.

Guesting on various TV shows, Cliff discussed religious beliefs with actor Hugh Lloyd, TV presenter Cathy McGowan, singer Paul Jones and Billy Graham.

Cliff's Summer of Love single was the Hank Marvin song, The Day I Met Marie and he was taken aback after being mobbed by fans. He said, 'I thought those days were over now.'

In September, Cliff spoke out about The Beatles: 'I think they are searching along the wrong track… The Beatles have said they are searching for God. There's only one way to find him…that's through Jesus Christ…meditation, like an LSD trip, is only a temporary thing. Christianity is something that is with you all the time.'

The month he turned 27, Cliff undertook concerts in Tokyo and was asked to be Britain's representative in the 1968 Eurovision Song Contest. His 40th single, All My Love was released in November and during one interview he discussed his sight problem: 'About a year ago I got some contact lenses and I just couldn't wear them. Recently I was told that some German lenses were the best in the world, so last week I went to Germany and had them fitted there. I don't see people when I haven't got glasses or contact lenses…I just see vague blurs.'

1968

During their Talk Of The Town season early in the year, Cliff demonstrated his versatility by taking over on drums for one night when Tony Meehan from The Shadows was taken ill with appendicitis.

In an interview with The Sunday Times Cliff said: 'I've lived for years with people saying I'm a poof, but I don't give a damn what they say. My best friends know me and that's all that matters. Even before I became a Christian I wasn't going to lay chicks just to prove myself.'

Cliff's involvement with Church matters became an increasingly significant part of his life, as he not only lent his name to Christian causes but got involved musically in the evangelical aspect of promoting his faith.

In February, Cliff shot the TV play A Matter Of Diamonds in which he played a young crook and received a reasonable critique from one reviewer: 'Normally I never fail to feel embarrassed at the sight of a young pop star attempting to become a serious actor, but Cliff has at last bridged the gap, and although "Riley Walker" was not the most taxing of roles, he coped competently.'

That same month, the final six Eurovision song contenders that he would be singing on Cilla Black's TV series were announced. They included songs from top writers Mike

Leander, Tony Hazzard, Roger Cook & Roger Greenaway, Tommy Scott, Guy Fletcher & Doug Flett and Bill Martin & Phil Coulter. It was the Martin-Coulter song Congratulations that eventually took the honours and would represent the UK, having polled 171,000 of the 250,000 votes. The song was released as Cliff's next single and featured The Ladybirds on backing vocals.

Cliff's new book, The Way It Is was published, one reviewer commenting, 'Cliff Richard, whether you think he's as nutty as a fruitcake or, as he really is, as nice as pie, is unquestionably doing a great job for his Saviour.'

Congratulations came second to the Spanish entry La, La, La by Massiel, but Cliff wasn't downhearted: 'Of course I'm disappointed, but it was so close I don't consider it any disgrace.' It would outsell the winner, globally by a colossal amount, with Cliff recording it for nearly every country in Europe and with 56 versions being released around the world. Co-writer Bill Martin commented: The ironic thing is that Germany, whose votes lost us the contest, have placed a 150,000 order.'

In April Cliff holidayed with The Crusaders on The Norfolk Broads, appeared on an Easter edition of Top Of The Pops and flew to Sweden to begin a three-country mini-evangelism tour.

May saw him appearing on an anniversary edition of Saturday Club, ATV's The Big Show, the NME Poll Winners Concert and beginning a season at The Talk of the Town, where he told the audience: 'I'm not becoming a monk and I'm not becoming a nun either, and I have no stained-glass window in my E-type.' He also spoke about his lack of consistent success in the United States: 'It just won't happen for me there and I won't change my career to make it. There was a time when things were pro-British over there and anything that was big in the chart here, automatically got away. I was somehow left behind. We decided about five years ago that we could gear our career to the States…yes, both The Shads and I are very tiny in America!'

June brought the Bratislava Song Contest, which he had to pull out of at the last moment, the premiere of Two A Penny, an appearance on The Billy Cotton Band Show, BBC2's Cliff Richard at the Talk of the Town, and the release of his 42nd single I'll Love You Forever Today. The following month Cliff flew to the States, combining film discussions with a holiday, taking in Sunset Strip, Las Vegas, Disneyland, Santa Barbara, San Francisco and Hollywood and was drawn into talking about The Beatles: 'They felt they had to say clever things in front of the press, but when John Lennon, for example, came out with that quote about The Beatles being more popular than Jesus Christ I regarded it as the height of childishness for a supposed adult cynic. I just feel that The Beatles are too ready to rush on to new sounds, but as people they've risen in my estimation because they try so hard to find something worthwhile out of life and when they find it's not the answer, they have the guts to say so…like with LSD and then with the Maharishi. If only they gave Christianity the same gusto…boy they'd find what they were seeking.'

In September, the NME added a special supplement to celebrate Cliff and The Shadows' 10th anniversary and Cliff was looking forward to his forthcoming A level in Religious Instruction to add to the O level he passed three years earlier at a hush-hush exam in Lewes. He was now assistant leader in The Crusaders Union, an interdenominational religious group and helped his friend Bill Latham raise money for various charities. In tandem with this side of his life, he also undertook a 12½ month autumn residency at the London Palladium, released his 43rd single, Marianne and appeared alongside The Shadows in a London Weekend TV Special, Cliff Richard at the Movies.

Hard on the heels of Marianne, Don't Forget To Catch Me was released and there followed a round of TV and radio appearances, including Off The Record, Songs Of Praise, The Morecambe & Wise Christmas Show and Top Of The Pops.

As the festive season approached, Cliff hit out at people's changing attitude to Christmas: 'People don't celebrate Christmas for the right reasons any more. To too many, Christmas is just a holiday…a booze-up time…although I've got nothing against boozing. They forget the fact that the only reason we celebrate it is because it's Christ's birthday.'

1969

Cliff got the New Year underway by performing a charity concert with The Settlers at the Royal Albert Hall and recorded 19 new songs at Abbey Road, 16 of which still remain unissued.

Voted Best-Dressed Male Star for the umpteenth time, Cliff said: 'I've got nothing against outrageous clothing… in fact if I'm invited to a party where they say "informal clothes", I think it's a great excuse to wear something extravagant like a pink frilly shirt!'

His 45th single, Good Times (Better Times) was released as he returned to Abbey Road Studios to record Don't Forget To Catch Me in Italian, German and French, appeared on Top Of The Pops and The Rolf Harris Show and then flew off to appear in Germany, Italy, Holland and Romania. On his return he guested on Liberace's TV show and Top Of The Pops.

Cliff talked about rumours of his retirement: 'I realise that if I quit, I'd be like a rat deserting a sinking ship. There are other Christians active in show business and it was partly due to some of them that I decided to stay in the business. There is nothing immoral or sordid about entertainment, providing that you don't allow yourself to be carried away by the glamour and financial rewards.'

On the subject of earnings he

revealed that he collected £15 in cash every Friday to see him through the week. 'Friday was always pay day for me and I think that unless you are paid in hard cash and actually see your money being spent, you can lose all sense of its value. My father raised our whole family on £11 a week.'

In May, Cliff appeared at the NME Poll Winners Concert and the music paper eulogised: 'His voice is wild, screaming with soul. This is Cliff on his greatest form, literally destroying any contention that his religious beliefs make him tame and goody-goody. There is no doubt that Cliff Richard is a phenomenon of British pop.'

That same month his 46th single Big Ship, written by Raymond Froggatt, was released and Cliff flew to the US to discuss a possible follow-up film to Two A Penny with Billy Graham.

In June, Cliff won two Ivor Novello Awards for Congratulations, appeared on Pete Murray's Pete's Saturday People and Top of The Pops twice.

In an interview, Hank Marvin said: 'Much of the credit for Cliff's staying power must go to the way in which his career has been guided by Peter Gormley, his manager…'

Cliff holidayed in Portugal and then on the Island of Herm in the Channel Islands, after discussing plans with the BBC for his own series the following year.

Cliff's 47th single Throw Down A Line was a duet with Hank Marvin, the pair appearing on Scene and Heard and Top Of The Pops twice.

In October, The Shadows reformed to back Cliff on a Japanese tour, with keyboard player Alan Hawkshaw augmenting the line-up. This was followed by a UK tour and Cliff's 48th single, With The Eyes Of A Child.

Talking about the actress Una Stubbs, Cliff said: 'She'd be my own personal Miss World. One of the most underestimated artists in the whole world too.'

It was announced by The Bromley Theatre Trust that Cliff would star in a stage version of Five Finger Exercise and also, along with The Shadows, do a stage musical version of Pinocchio for Christmas 1970.

It was a Cliff-fest December: Cliff appeared on the Cilla Black Show, Christmas With Cliff, Let's Go With Cliff, Pop Go The Sixties and LWTV screened The Young Ones.

1970

The year began with the first of 13 shows in the BBC TV series It's Cliff Richard. Into the new decade Cliff confessed: 'I think my acting is the direction my career must improve in…I can't see my voice improving any more and if I didn't have anything more to strive for I might be in danger of getting stale.'

In January, Cliff was voted Korea's Top Singer and received an award from the Songwriters' Guild of Great Britain for 'The Most Outstanding Service To Music in 1969.'

Cliff's 49th single, The Joy Of Living again featured Hank Marvin.

In March, Cliff attended a party given by the Prime Minister, Harold Wilson, in honour of the West German Chancellor, Willy Brandt.

In the spring, a book entitled Cliff Richard–Questions was published in which he sounded off on various topics. On Eurovision he said that 'the voting was right up the spout', on girlfriends, 'I don't see how you can have a really close relationship with a girl unless you marry her' and on racialism, 'no one race or skin colour is better than another in God's sight'.

It was a bearded Cliff that appeared at the NME Poll Winners Concert, as he was growing it for his role in Five Finger Exercise, which opened later that month.

Cliff's milestone 50th single was Goodbye Sam, Hello Samantha, the release being celebrated by a party,

Left: Left to right: Cilla Black, Cliff Richard and Lulu at the 'Disc and Music Echo' Valentine Awards ceremony at the Cafe Royal in London, 13th February 1970.

attended by many luminaries including Radio One's John Peel! In an interview Cliff admitted that his favourite of all the 50 singles was The Day I Met Marie.

In the summer, Cliff flew to South Africa at the invitation of The Bishop of Natal to speak and sing in Durban at a series of youth meetings.

Journalist Andy Gray put in print why he felt that Cliff had outlasted all his rivals: 'Cliff has always been so generous and friendly with everyone. You never hear of him having a feud or a disagreement or being nasty to anyone. His public relations are perfect…he has never forgotten that it is the fans who have made him and retained him. He has been an inspiration to thousands who have chosen faith in Christ as their way of life.'

August saw the release of the 51st single, I Ain't Got Time Anymore, prior to a four-week season at London's Talk Of The Town.

Just before his 30th birthday he was presented with the National Viewers And Listeners Award for 'Outstanding Contribution to Religious Broadcasting and Light Entertainment'.

On a two-week tour of the UK Cliff was backed by Marvin, Welch and Farrar. In one interview on tour he was described as being 'mechanically polite,' to which he responded: …'What really stung was the realisation that here was somebody knocking me for trying to be pleasant and friendly.'

1971

Sunny Honey Girl became Cliff's 52nd single as the series It's Cliff Richard got under way. The series would feature such artists as Marvin, Welch and Farrar, The New Seekers, Petula Clark and Elton John.

The series was followed by a tour of Holland, appearances in Denmark, Germany, Austria, Switzerland and Belgium and the 53rd single, Silvery Rain.

In May, Cliff appeared in the play The Potting Shed at the Bromley New Theatre and plans were announced for his next film, Xanadu, which was to be shot on location in Newcastle. Producer Andrew Mitchell commented: 'This will not be a sugar sweet out-and-out musical. Basically it's the tale of a romance in an industrial city.'

The 54th single, Flying Machine was released in June. It became his first single not to make the top 30, but reached the No 1 spot in Denmark and Malaysia. During the summer, he collected an Ivor Novello Award for 'Outstanding Services To British Music' and recorded Get Away With Cliff for BBC1 with Olivia Newton-John, Hank Marvin, Bruce Welch and John Farrar, who also joined him for a three-week London Palladium show in the autumn, which would break box-office records.

The shooting of Xanadu was

postponed until the following year and Cliff's 55th single Sing A Song Of Freedom was banned in South Africa because of political repression.

At the end of the year, Cliff spoke about Christmas: 'You have to remember that the majority of people don't believe in Christ, and Christmas is about Christianity. It certainly doesn't worry me that it's commercial...because I don't celebrate it in a commercial way.'

1972

Another series of It's Cliff Richard got under way on the BBC, with appearances over the 13-week period, including resident artists such as Olivia Newton-John and The Flirtations. Una Stubbs was expecting a baby and was replaced on the first show by Dandy Nicholls. Other guests during the series included, Labi Siffre, Elton John and The New Seekers.

In the NME poll, Cliff won the British Vocal Personality and British Male Singer sections, came second to Elvis in the World Music Personality section and third in the Best TV/Radio Show with It's Cliff Richard.

In February, Cliff's 56th single, Jesus, was released after which he appeared at a Tear Fund concert in Manchester, a gospel concert in Liverpool and supported a national young people's Help The Police competition.

Cliff won The Sun newspaper's Top Male Pop Personality for the third year running.

During the summer, Cliff toured dozens of countries in Europe, the Middle East and the Far East and released his 57th single, Living In Harmony.

In September, BBC2 screened The Case, a comedy thriller which included eight songs and starred Cliff, Olivia Newton-John and Tim Brooke-Taylor.

In October, backed by the Brian Bennett Orchestra, Cliff undertook a

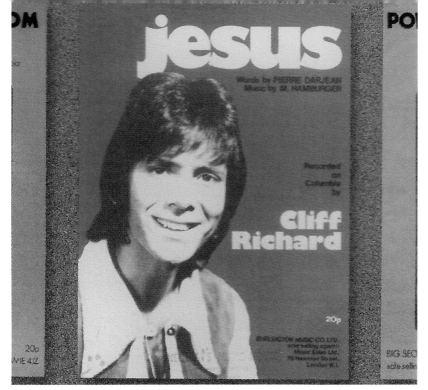

Left: Promotional Handbill for Cliff's 1972 single *Jesus*. This was his first religious single and it was to become his worst-selling record to date.

26-date tour of the UK, which was followed by an appearance on the BBC2 TV Special 50 Years of Music, alongside Vera Lynn, Henry Hall, Gilbert O'Sullivan, Lulu and The New Seekers.

Cliff's 58th single, A Brand New Song was released in December and became his first-ever single not to

chart, as it failed to reach the top 50.

Cliff said: 'I really can't understand why. I played it to my mother and she was sure it would be a hit. In the run-up to Christmas Cliff performed at a special concert to raise money for the Arts Centre Group (The ACG), and appeared at Batley Variety Club.

1973

Early in 1973, Cliff appeared on Belgium TV with Cliff In Scotland as well as appearing on Cilla Black's BBC TV series performing songs for Eurovision and began a three-week residency at London's Talk Of The Town.

In an interview Cliff said: 'Mary Whitehouse is 10 years ahead of her time…the cinema medium is being wasted. Morally something has got to be done about it. There's a need for censorship.'

Power To All Our Friends, the song chosen to represent the UK in the Eurovision Song Contest, became Cliff's 59th single release. The song, written by Guy Fletcher

and Doug Flett became Cliff's first top 10 hit since Goodbye Sam, Hello Samantha in 1970.

In an interview with the News Of The World Cliff admitted: 'In the past two or three years I've not dated many girls at all…at the moment there's no-one I want to date.'

The Eurovision Contest was held in Luxembourg and 300 million people from 32 countries saw Cliff come third, with Luxembourg's Anne-Marie David winning with Tu Te reconnoitres (Wonderful Dream).

Cliff wasn't enamoured with the result: 'I just don't like the winning

song…no, it's not sour grapes.'

In April and May, he appeared in concerts across Australia as part of an evangelistic crusade under the banner of Help, Hope and Hallelujah and it was announced that in June he would make his first feature film since Finders Keepers.

The film's working title, Hot Property, soon changed to Take Me High and he and his co-stars including George Cole, Anthony Andrews and Debbie Watling began shooting in Birmingham just as Cliff's 60th single, Help It Along was released. This was actually an EP containing the remaining four Eurovision contenders.

In the late summer Cliff appeared at two concerts with Johnny Cash, at Earls Court with Spriritual Re-emphasis and at Wembley Stadium.

In November, Take Me High was premiered in London with Cliff playing the role of young merchant banker Tim Matthews. The title track became his 61st single.

The good reviews were tempered by the death of Shadows' bass player John Rostill.

1974

Far Right:
Promotional poster
for the film Take
Me High of which
the sound track
was released in
1974.

At the beginning of January, Cliff played his first game of football for almost 20 years when he turned out for the Buzz All Stars against a Choralerna XI. Buzz being a British Christian youth journal and Choralerna, a Swedish Christian choir.

For much of February Cliff was in Abbey Road recording and the following month received the Silver Clef trophy for outstanding services to music from the Duchess of Gloucester.

April saw a season at the London Palladium after which his 62nd single, You Keep Me Hanging On was released and Cliff performed it on various TV and Radio programmes, including the Nana Mouskouri Show, and the Mike Yarwood Show.

In Cheshunt, Cliff appeared as Bottom in his old school's production of A Midsummer Night's Dream.

During the summer, The International Cliff Richard Movement met in London with Cliff answering members' questions and two films being shown: Love Never Gives Up and A Day In The Life Of Cliff Richard.

In the late summer/early autumn BBC screened a new series

of It's Cliff Richard, he appeared at a special concert in London for The Crusaders and lent his support to the Romsey Abbey appeal.

At the end of October he undertook a series of gospel dates after which Cliff and The Shadows reunited for a charity concert at the London Palladium which resulted in the group being invited to sing the United Kingdom's six Eurovision song possibilities for 1975.

A soundtrack album for the film Take Me High by Richard was issued and remains in print to this day. It features songs performed by Cliff in the film as well as the duets he performed with various other cast members. The title cut was a UK top 30 single for Cliff.

During November, Tories in Scotland, using Sing A Song Of Freedom for their campaign, were told that they must pay performing rights and Cliff opened a Christian bookshop in Sutton.

From November 7th through to December 14th Cliff undertook a 23-date tour of the UK.

1975

Far Right: Cliff from a photo shoot in early 1975.

Early in 1975, Cliff performed with Swedish Christian choir Choralerna at Manchester, Newcastle and Leicester and at the Name of Jesus concert at the Royal Albert Hall.

In March, Cliff's 63rd single, It's Only Me You've Left Behind, was released but failed to chart despite appearances on Saturday Scene and the Bay City Rollers' TV Show, Shang-a-Lang.

The following month Cliff talked about his faith at the Way To Life rally at Wembley's Empire Pool and performed three songs. Part of the rally was covered by BBC Radio 4.

The summer saw Cliff at a charity concert in Manchester, appearing on the TV show Jim'll Fix It, and appearing at a lunch to honour Vera Lynn.

In September, a new BBC series called It's Cliff and Friends began and Cliff's 64th single Honky Tonk Angel was released, although he would later withdraw his support for it after realising the song referred to a prostitute.

Interviewed on ITV's Today programme, he declared that he had no idea that a 'honky tonk angel' was a prostitute until somebody told him while he was in America. He said that he hadn't intended to upset anyone and that if DJs didn't want to play it he wouldn't particularly mind.

Later he said: 'I hope it's a flop. I never want to hear it again and I hope most of the public never hear it. Now I know what I've been singing about I've taken steps to do all I can to make it a flop I hope no-one buys it. If the record is a hit and I'm asked to sing it, I will refuse unless the words are changed.' In the 2000s he would re-appraise the song more kindly and admitted that it might be worth re-visiting.

Whilst critics had been pointing out that Cliff's career was in the doldrums singles-wise, a sea-change was taking place in the studio, with three studio sessions at Abbey Road yielding Devil Woman and Miss You Nights.

December brought more recording sessions, mainly for the Bruce Welch-produced album, I'm Nearly Famous, recordings for Radio One and Radio Two's Gospel Road series and a Christmas Day special for BBC Radio.

1976

Miss You Nights became Cliff's 65th single and his first of 1976, the song taking him into the singles chart for the first time since July 1974.

In April, religious organisation, Scope, staged two charity concerts featuring Cliff and Larry Norman in aid of the National Institute for the Healing of Addictions.

Miss You Nights was followed up by Devil Woman, with one reviewer asking; 'Has Cliff been caught out again? He cut a previous single, Honky Tonk Angel, without apparently knowing what it was about. This time someone may have forgotten to tell him what the words 'devil' and 'woman' mean. You see Cliffie, a "devil" is a naughty person and a "woman" is more or less a person of the opposite sex. Now, is it right for an upstanding young man to sing about naughtiness and sex?'

Following promotion in Holland, Luxembourg, local ILR stations and on Radio One, a Hong Kong newspaper printed a bizarre piece of editorial under the heading, Cliff Richard Circus Is Coming To Town: 'Clifford Richard Hong Kong's golden boy and Great Britain's answer to Black Oak Arkansas is expected for concert dates in Hong Kong some time in June according to L'artiste's recording labelle, EMI. Clifford, the controversial heavy metal gun of rock,

known for his bizarre stage regalia and electic cynicism is rumoured to be bringing with him, 1,500 watt strobe lights, the Bolshoi Ballet and a herd of performing elephants,'

(Before you write to the publisher, all punctuation and spelling mistakes belong to the Hong Kong newspaper!)

During June and July Cliff appeared on such programmes as Supersonic, BBC2's Cliff In Concert and Top Of The Pops. Devil Woman started to pick up heavy airplay in the US and gave him his third–ever Stateside hit single and his first since 1964.

The summer brought the release of his 67th single, I Can't Ask For Anymore Than You, and appearances on Nationwide, Thames TV and across the States promoting Devil Woman.

Most of September was taken up with recording at Abbey Road, with a UK tour following immediately.

In November, Cliff discussed the Tear Fund charity at length, explaining that it had been set up eight or nine years earlier to provide money for Third World projects.

During November and December Cliff performed at the Royal Albert Hall, released his 68th single Hey Mr Dream Maker, performed in Delhi, met Mother Teresa of Calcutta and visited the homes for the destitute and dying.

1977

Far Right: The
book Which One's
Cliff?

January was mainly taken up with recording secular songs for the album Small Corners.

The Cliff Richard Movement magazine, Dynamite, revealed that Cliff's Tear Fund concerts in 1976 raised over £37,000, the money provided six vehicles for Argentina, The Yemen Arab Republic, Nigeria, Haiti and Burundi as well as a generator for a hospital in India, a rural development centre in Kenya and a nutritional training centre in Zaire.

Following the release of the 69th single, My Kinda Life, one reviewer looked back at the last year: 'Besides being a neat riposte to America's apparent indifference, the I'm Nearly Famous album had an entirely deserved regenerative effect on Cliff's career.'

Following the TH and Radio promotion for My Kinda Life, Cliff toured Australia and New Zealand before returning to take part in the Queen's Silver Jubilee celebrations by speaking at a youth rally in Windsor Great Park.

On the subject of punk rock Cliff commented: 'The punks think they own the pop scene, but they forget they're just leasing it from us…what we've got going now is the first generation of 40 year olds who dig rock & roll. When I was 18, people of 40 hated rock. Now when we're 60, it may sound ridiculous, but I'm going to love rock, the music will still be our music.'

In June, Cliff promoted his 70th single, When Two Worlds Drift Apart, on Top Of The Pops and Saturday Scene before holidaying at his house in Portugal.

The book Which One's Cliff? was published. The book was written by Cliff in conjunction with Bill Latham and dealt with his career and religious beliefs.

The book launch was followed by a tour of Europe, before he returned to appear on DLT's Radio One show, Tiswas and Michael Parkinson's TV chat show ahead of a UK gospel tour.

In his 37th birthday month he collected two awards, Best British Male Artist and the Gold Badge Award from The Songwriter's Guild of Great Britain.

In December a reunion with The Shadows was announced for a series of concerts at the London Palladium the following spring.

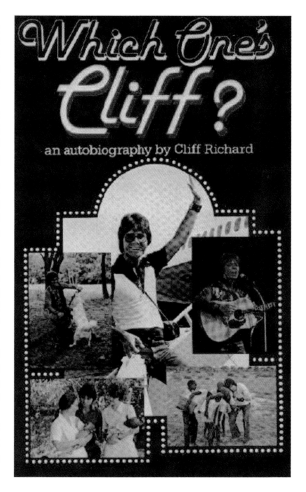

1978

January was mainly taken up with Abbey Road recording sessions for the Green Light album, during which Cliff's 71st single, Yes, He Lives was released, but failed to chart. In February, he appeared on Pebble Mill At One, and in a concert for the Arts Centre Group, before playing the two-week reunion concert with The Shadows at the London Palladium.

In March and April there were more recording sessions for Green Light and the live recordings from the Palladium shows.

In June, Cliff attended the opening of the ACG's new headquarters near London's Old Vic, while on the music front, his 72nd single Please Remember Me was released. Like the previous single it didn't chart.

The summer brought a tour of South Africa, Australia and Hong Kong, before he returned to join evangelist Dick Saunders on stage and appeared on German TV.

In October, BBC Radio 1 broadcast the first in a five-part series entitled Twenty Golden Years, which traced Cliff's career and was narrated by Tim Rice. Also that month, under the banner of Help, Hope & Hallelujah, Cliff gave two concerts to celebrate the 10th anniversary of Tear Fund.

Since his initial donation of two

concerts in 1969, he had undertaken a national tour, become a member of the board, narrated three promotional trips and visited the Fund's projects in Sudan, Nepal and Bangladesh.

In an interview about Tear Fund Cliff said: 'You know, it never fails to encourage me when I think that at this very moment, somewhere in the world a Christian is using an x-ray unit or driving a Land Rover or even a building paid for by one of these concerts.'

In November, Cliff attended a party in London's Belgrave Square for the launch of the first Guinness Book Of British Hit Singles, along with fellow artists that included, Elton John, Johnny Ray, Bob Geldof, Vera Lynn, Kate Bush, Errol Brown, Hank Marvin, Russ Conway and The Drifters. A photograph was taken for the cover of the second book.

That same month Can't Take The Hurt Anymore became Cliff's 73rd single.

1979

At the beginning of the year, the UK Scripture Union launched a series of cassettes which featured Cliff reading from the scriptures, and EMI threw a lunch for Cliff at Claridge's to celebrate their 21-year partnership where they presented him with a gold replica of the key to their Manchester Square headquarters.

At the Music Week Awards, Cliff and The Shadows received an award for 21 years as major British recording artists.

In February and March, there was more recording at Abbey Road for the album Rock & Roll Juvenile, and Green Light, became Cliff's 74th single.

During the spring he recorded for Dutch TV, took part in a youth festival at St Albans Cathedral and attended the Local Radio awards.

The summer saw Cliff taking part in Bible readings for the Scripture Union and attending the European Baptist Congress, where he talked about his work with Tear Fund and his visits to the Soviet Union.

In July, he was guest of honour at a Variety Club of Great Britain lunch, which was celebrating his 21 years in show business and his 75th single was released.

We Don't Talk Anymore, written by Alan Tarney, took Cliff back to the No 1 spot for the first time since Congratulations.

In August, Cliff launched his own gospel label, Patch, and performed a 90-minute set at the Greenbelt Festival. He later attended a Christian Holiday Crusade meeting at Filey, where he took part in discussions and signed books. Cliff also took part in Hosannah 79, an anti-racist festival held in Birmingham.

September saw one Webb depose another at the top of the chart, when the former Harry Webb's We Don't Talk Anymore was knocked of by the former Gary Webb's Cars.

Hot Shot became Cliff's 76th single, as We Don't Talk Anymore became the fourth of his singles to enter the US Top 40, eventually making the top 10.

In December in an event hosted by Mike Read, Cliff performed in front of the Queen, Prince Charles and thousands of young people to mark the end of the Year of the Child.

Left: 14th
November 1979:
British pop singer
Kate Bush joins
Cliff Richard,
Labi Siffre,
Russell Harty and
members of the
London Symphony
Orchestra.

1980

The year got underway with an interview on US TV about Cliff's OBE and his American career ,followed by an appearance on the Dinah Shore TV Show. In the UK, his 77th single, Carrie was released and Cliff appeared at a tribute concert for Norrie Paramor, his long-time producer who had passed away the previous September.

That same month he attended a 'Christians IN Sport' dinner, took part in an evangelist meeting with Billy Graham and received the award for 'Best Family Entertainer' at the Radio 1, Daily Mirror and Nationwide National Rock & Pop Awards. (This was the first of the awards that eventually became The Brits.)

In the spring Cliff appeared in two episodes of ITV's Pop Gospel series, was voted Top Pop Star on Noel Edmonds TV show Swap Shop and won the TV Times award for 'The Most Exciting Male Singer on Television.'

Cliff also appeared at London's Royal Albert Hall at the 'Sing The Good News' event, honouring the top writers in a contest organised by the Bible Society.

In April, Carrie became the fifth big stateside hit and Capital Radio listener Kim Keyne bid £1,400 to have lunch with Cliff.

July heralded a gospel tour and a trip to Buckingham Palace to collect his OBE. He was presented to the

Queen dressed in a black suit, red tie, red rose and bright red trainers: 'I haven't got any morning dress, so I thought I'd wear something colourful! I've been to the Palace before and I knew there was a lot of red about the place. I have always been a firm Royalist and have followed the Royal Family since I was a kid.'

In the summer, Cliff appeared in Germany with his new group, the Sky Band, released his 78th single, Dreamin' and read biblical texts for the BBC world service programme Reflections.

During the month of his 40th birthday, he undertook a five-night show at London's Apollo Theatre, which was recorded by the BBC, appeared on Swap Shop and released his 79th single, Suddenly, a duet with Olivia Newton-John.

December saw Cliff performing on the Michael Parkinson Show and designing a festive window for London store, Selfridges. He opted for a traditional religious theme, Christmas Through The Eyes of a Child.

1981

A Little In Love became Cliff's 80th single and also provided him with another top 20 hit in the US, peaking while he was over there promoting his forthcoming tour. His appearances included Los Angeles TV shows, the John Kelly Show, the John Davidson Show, the Merv Griffin Show and the Dionne Warwick Solid Gold Show. He also travelled to New York and Canada to do more promotion.

On his return to London, he attended the 25th birthday celebrations of the evangelical magazine, Crusade, where he talked about his recent American trip, his forthcoming concerts and the death of John Lennon.

The first meetings that would lay the foundation for the musical Time took place at the end of January with producer Dave Clark.

The February schedule included Top Of The Pops, The Kenny Everett Show, Crusaders meetings, and fund-raising for St. Brendan's School, Bristol as headmaster John Davey had helped Cliff to pass his O level in Religious Studies in 1965. That month there was also a 'Christians In Sport' dinner and the Daily Mirror Readers' Award for 'Outstanding Musical Personality of the Year,' which was presented to him by Una Stubbs. At the end of February, Cliff flew to Canada and the United States for the start of a month-long tour, which took in 32 venues, including Seattle, Minneapolis, Milwaukee, Denver, San Francisco, Los Angeles, Chicago, Ottawa, Toronto and Montreal,

Give A Little Bit More was released as a single in the States where it made the Top 40.

While he was away, his first UK video, The Young Ones was released and BBC TV screens Cliff In London.

After his return, at the end of April, he starred in a 'Rock Special' at the Hammersmith Odeon which would form the basis of a BBC programme with interviews from many show business colleagues, including Marty Wilde, Adam Faith and The Shadows.

Cliff shot a video for his new single at Milton Keynes before holidaying in Portugal, South Africa and Mauritius.

In August, his 81st single Wired For Sound was released and promoted on Top Of The Pops and Get It Together. Two gospel shows at Wembley were followed by a week in Wales and a fortnight in New York and Los Angeles.

The autumn included German

Left: 3rd May 1981: Cliff performing at London's Hard Rock Cafe for a BBC documentary about the 1950's rock 'n' roll scene.

TV, The Royal Variety Show and a four-part series entitled Cliff which looked at his 23 years in the business. The mini-series covered his gospel concerts, charity work, religion and life on the road as well as interviews with business and personal friends.

The press were intrigued as Cliff and Sue Barker begin to see each other regularly.

In November, Cliff's 82nd single, Daddy's Home was released, having sung it live on stage and declaring the Shep and the Limelites original as one of the favourites on his own juke box.

Cliff recorded the Christmas edition of Pop Quiz before flying off to spend the holiday in Florida.

1982

The year got underway with Cliff being interviewed by eight Australian newspapers and nine Australian radio stations over a period of 14 hours.

In February, Cliff set off on a world tour, commencing in Bangkok, Singapore and Hong Kong, before going on to Australia, New Zealand and the United States.

Cliff teamed up with Weetabix to raise money for underprivileged children, assisted with Capital Radio's 'Help A London Child', undertook several local newspaper interviews and visited Northern Ireland.

In May, Cliff visited Kenya with Bill Latham on behalf of Tear Fund and on his return opened a new Dr Barnardo's home in Wokingham.

Cliff's 83rd single, The Only Way Out, was released in July as Cliff flew to the States and Canada for another tour.

A holiday in Bermuda followed the tour and in September his 84th single Where Do We Go From Here was released.

In October, Cliff and Phil Everly recorded She Means Nothing To Me at Eden Studios, the session being produced by Stuart Colman and featuring Mark Knopfler.

A European and Scandinavian tour followed, he filmed a Christmas record token commercial for EMI and attended the 'Christians In Sport' dinner.

Chris Eaton's re-working of the carol O Little Town of Bethlehem, was released as Little Town and was Cliff's 85th single.

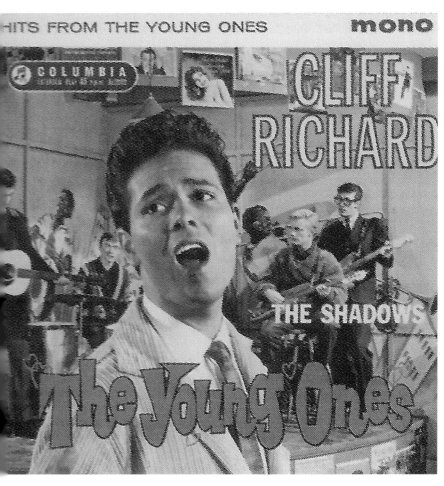

HITS FROM THE YOUNG ONES

mono

COLUMBIA

CLIFF RICHARD

THE SHADOWS

The Young Ones

Left: In 1982 the British sitcom The Young Ones was first broadcast. The series' theme song featured the cast singing Cliff Richard and The Shadows' UK No. 1 song "The Young Ones".

1983

In January, the film Cliff in Kenya was premiered at BAFTA in London's Piccadilly, he took part in a tennis tournament in Holland and presented a cheque to the Great Ormond Street Children's Hospital as part of the Weetabix campaign.

The duet with Phil Everly, She Means Nothing To Me, was released in February and reached the top 10.

Late in March, Cliff recorded at Air Studios with Mike Batt and attended a memorial service at St Martin-in-the-Fields for comedian Arthur Askey.

Most of April was taken up with a European and Scandinavian tour that included Lisbon, Barcelona, Antwerp, Brussels, Rotterdam and Malmo.

His 87th UK single, a re-working of Buddy Holly's True Love Ways was also released that month, with Drifting, a duet with Sheila Walsh, following hard on its heels.

During the summer, Lord Snowdon photographed Cliff in a four-hour session, he recorded Pop Quiz and the BBC's Time Of Your Life, watched the tennis finals at Wimbledon, and flew to Holland with Billy Graham for an International conference.

After a holiday in Portugal, Never Say Die was released, becoming Cliff's 89th single and he appeared at the Greenbelt Christian Festival.

In September, Cliff sent a telegram to The Shadows at their Silver Luncheon,

congratulating them on 25 years in the business.

As part of his 43rd birthday celebrations, Cliff co-hosted the Radio One Breakfast Show live from Mike Read's house.

The October and November schedule included a charity lunch with Princess Anne, the 'Tin Pan Alley Ball,' and appearances at The Apollo, which was watched by Olivia Newton-John, Princess Anne, Tim Rice, Princess Alexandra, and Angus Ogilvy.

Cliff's 90th single, Mike Batt's Please Don't Fall In Love was released and reaches the top 10.

There was also tennis for TVAM at David Lloyd's Tennis Centre and Cliff's inaugural pro-celebrity tennis tournament at Brighton with Sue Barker, Trevor Eve, Hank Marvin, Jo Durie, Anne Hobbs, Sue Mappin and Mike Read.

1984

At the beginning of the year Cliff holidayed in Portugal and spent time in the States, the Far East and Scandinavia.

Cliff's 92nd single, Baby You're Dynamite, was released and peaked at No 27.

The fans and radio stations however clearly preferred the B side, Ocean Deep and the DJs began to favour that side. EMI belatedly flipped the single and begin promoting Ocean Deep, but it was too late to have the impact it might have done had it been the original A side. Ocean Deep will repeatedly win the fans vote year on year as their all-time favourite

Cliff song.

In April, Cliff and Bill Latham travelled to Haiti, where they visited Port-au- Prince and La Gonave, the latter inspiring Cliff to write a song about his visit there. Two months later he would record the song at Gallery Studios for the album The Rock Connection.

In the early summer he filmed for the Golden Rose of Montreux festival, attended a service at Westminster Abbey for 'Christian Heritage Year,' a 'Mission To London' Christian evening and recorded for BBC TV's Rock Gospel Show.

After another holiday in Portugal

Cliff undertook a nine-date tour of the UK with The Shadows in July and recorded more tracks for The Rock Connection at Strawberry Studios South in Dorking.

Following an earlier meeting between Peter Gormley and Dave Clark, Cliff and Dave met to discuss the musical Time.

The September schedule includes a UK gospel tour, filming at the David Lloyd Tennis Centre and the 92nd single, Two To The Power, a duet with Janet Jackson.

On his 44th birthday, Cliff flew to Australia for The Rock Connection tour of Australia and New Zealand, which included Perth, Brisbane, Sydney, Canberra, Melbourne, Adelaide, Auckland and Wellington.

While he was away EMI released the 93rd single, Shooting From The Heart, but it failed to make the top 50.

In December Cliff attended the silver wedding of Shadows' drummer, Brian Bennett and his wife Margaret, recorded at the BBC for a Rock Gospel Christmas special and recorded for Mike Yarwood's

Christmas show.

On the 15th Cliff staged his second pro-celebrity tennis tournament, featuring top British tennis players and Hank Marvin, Terry Wogan and Mike Yarwood.

After attending the Arts Centre Group's carol service he flew off to South Africa for three weeks.

Above: Cliff released his 92nd single, Two To The Power, a duet with Janet Jackson.

1985

Far Right: Virginia Wade played with Cliff during the pro-celebrity tennis tournament of 1985.

On his return from South Africa his 94th single, Heart User was released, but stalled outside the top 40, despite appearances on The Tube, Aspel and Friends and Saturday Superstore.

During March and April Cliff recorded at the BBC for an Easter special, attended a reception at 10 Downing Street and holidayed in Portugal.

In the spring he played in a pro-celebrity tennis tournament, filmed for Jim'll Fix It and attended the launch of Mike Read's Pop Quiz board game at Stringfellows in London.

In May, he took part in LWT's 40 years of Peace at London's Palace Theatre, a health film for BBC Wales and attended a presentation lunch for the Guinness Book of Hit Singles at The Savoy, that included Adam Faith, David Cassidy, Bob Geldof, Lonnie Donegan, Vera Lynn and Hank Marvin.

In June, Ken Russell shoots the video for Cliff's forthcoming single, She's So Beautiful in the Lake District, Cliff dines at The House of Commons and attends a service for 'Christians In Sport.'

July saw Cliff on a UK gospel tour that included the Channel Islands. While there, Cliff and Bill Latham spent a day on the island of Herm, where they'd camped with The Crusaders in the late sixties.

After a few days in the USA, Cliff holidayed in Portugal before filming in Norway for a TV gala and attending a Polish youth conference in Warsaw.

In September, Cliff's 95th single, She's So Beautiful was released. The song, which reached No 17 in the chart, was from the musical Time and refers to the planet earth not a female.

During the same month he undertook press and radio promotion for Germany, Belgium, Holland and Denmark as well as appearing on Saturday Superstore and spending three days at Bisham Abbey with the 'Cliff Richard Tennis Hunt.'

In November and December, there were concerts in England and Scotland and the 96th single, It's In Every One Of Us, another song from Time, was released.

In the run-up to Christmas there were appearances on Pebble Mill at One and Saturday Superstore and the third annual pro-celebrity tennis tournament which again featured top tennis players including Annabel Croft and Virginia Wade partnering Shakin' Stevens, Hank Marvin and Mike Read.

1986

In January, Cliff attended the funeral of his drummer Graham Jarvis, before flying off for a break in Miami.

Later in the month Cliff began dancing lessons at Pineapple Studios in London in preparation for his role in Time and shot a video with the cast of the TV comedy series, The Young Ones for his next single.

During February there were more dancing lessons with Arlene Philips at Danceworks, he recorded She's So Beautiful for the TV Times Awards Show, and records another song from Time, It's In Every One Of Us for the TV show Aspel and Friends.

Cliff's 97th single, a reworked version of Living Doll, featured the cast of the TV comedy series The Young Ones and Hank Marvin.

His promotion for the Comic Relief single included an interview for the Daily Express with David Wigg, Reporting London and Saturday Superstore.

At the end of March, previews for the musical Time with Cliff playing the role of Chris Wilder...Rock Star, began at London's Dominion Theatre with the Duchess of Kent attending the charity evening in aid of Cancer Research. Living Doll became Cliff's 11th No 1 single, nearly 27 years after it first topped the chart.

As well as being on stage every night, during the spring Cliff also presented a Blue Peter award, attended a centenary service at St Paul's, Finchley, helped Sport Aid, opened a home for the mentally handicapped and attended the funeral of Bill Latham's mother, Mamie.

On the business front, he was interviewed live on Good Morning America with Dave Clark and undertook many local radio interviews with UK stations.

Born To Rock and Roll became Cliff's 98th single and the third to be released from the musical Time as Living Doll reached No 1 in Australia.

Cliff launched his new tennis project, Search For A Star, at the Dominion Theatre and did a workout for Sport Aid.

In June, Cliff attended a matinee of David Essex's new musical, Mutiny on the Bounty, saw the tennis at Wimbledon on most days and was a guest at a party thrown by Freddie Mercury.

In August, Cliff escaped with a bruised back as his Golf GTi aquaplaned on the M4 as he was travelling from the David Lloyd Tennis Centre at Heston to perform at The Dominion. The national press naturally played up the accident, using such terms as 'miracle M4 car escape', 'miracle crash escape,' 'Cliff Richard walks out of car wreck' and 'Cliff Richard's crash escape.'

In September, Cliff was at Bisham Abbey with aspiring young tennis players taking part in his Search For A Star project and his 99th single, All I Ask Of You, was released. The song, from Andrew Lloyd Webber's musical, Phantom of the Opera, was a duet with Sarah Brightman.

In October, Sir Laurence Olivier, who was represented by a hologram in Time, came to see the show and received a standing ovation. That same month, Cliff recorded Cliff From The Hip TV show for which he recorded two songs with Elton John, Slow Rivers and Leather Jackets and attended the launch of Mike Read's book The Cliff Richard File at what was the old 2i's coffee bar.

In November, Cliff attended Westminster Council's anti-drugs lunch where he signed a 'say no to drugs' plaque along with such artists as Bill Wyman, Julian Lennon and Dire Straits and afterwards lunched with the Princess of Wales.

Prior to Christmas he performed with Alvin Stardust, Dana and Roy Castle at the ACG carol concert, which was recorded by the BBC, as well as hosting his fourth annual pro-celebrity tennis tournament, which included Peter Cook, and Ronnie Corbett.

1987

In January, Cliff recorded Jim'll Fix It, Wogan and Good Morning Sunday as well as attending Anthony Andrews' birthday party.

Cliff went to see several houses with a view to moving home and in March was interviewed on BBC Breakfast Time with David Cassidy who was set to take over from him in Time.

In April, Cliff headed off for a break before launching his pro-celebrity tennis sponsorship at the Savoy Hotel, London and undertook a two-hour sitting for Madame Tussaud's.

The video for Cliff's next single, My Pretty One, was shot at Albert Wharf on the Thames after which Cliff had a short break in Portugal before starting rehearsals for his next tour, at Wimbledon Theatre and attending Sir Laurence Olivier's' birthday celebrations at the National Theatre.

Ahead of his gospel tour, which took in Newcastle, Edinburgh, Brighton, Wembley and Birmingham, Cliff was interviewed by Smash Hits, The Sun, the South London News, LBC and Capital Radio.

My Pretty One was released in June as Cliff gave a charity concert at Wimbledon Theatre, recorded the Roxy TV show in Newcastle and participated in It's A Knockout with Prince Edward and the Duchess of York. Also in June, Cliff viewed 'Charters' in Weybridge

that would become his new home, appeared on TV shows Wogan, Get Fresh, Top Of The Pops, Midlands Today, Hold Tight and The Edna Everage TV Show.

July saw a reunion party for the cast of Summer Holiday, German TV and TV South's Summertime Special for which he sang Summer Holiday, Some People and My Pretty One.

August was fairly hectic, with a holiday in Brindisi, the release of My Pretty One, the launch of the new album, Always Guaranteed and moving house to Charters in St George's Hill.

The following month there was more German TV, Norwegian TV,

Danish TV, the EMI world conference at Brighton and a Top Of The Pops pre-record and video shoot for his next single, Remember Me.

During September, October and November there was a 49-concert European tour, which included Hamburg, Berlin, Brussels, Rotterdam, Frankfurt, Zurich, Munich, Budapest, Zagreb, Belgrade, Bergen, Oslo, Stockholm, Helsinki and Copenhagen during which time the next single, Remember Me was released.

This year's annual pro-celebrity tennis tournament included Sue Barker, Virginia Wade, Elton John and Emlyn Hughes.

1988

The New Year brought a tour of Australia and New Zealand, taking in such cities as Christchurch, Wellington, Auckland, Perth, Adelaide, Brisbane, Sydney, Hobart, Melbourne, Canberra and Darwin, which finished towards the end of March.

While he was away, the new single, Two Hearts, was released.

Ahead of another European tour, Cliff undertook an enormous amount of press, TV and Radio promotion as well as opening a new channel at County Sound Radio, hosting a tennis fun day at Beckenham and singing When I Survey The Wondrous Cross for a BBC schools programme.

The European tour took place throughout May, this time including Oslo, Copenhagen, Rotterdam, Cologne, Stuttgart, Dusseldorf, Hamburg and Odense.

The summer schedule included Spanish TV, Danish TV, a programme for Singapore Airlines, an interview with Woman magazine and a photograph session for his new album.

As the book Single-Minded was published, Cliff gave interviews to a dozen local radio stations, Radio Radio, Radio Luxembourg, LBC and Anne Robinson for Radio Two.

During September he attended EMI's regional press day and European

Left: Cliff with the Ivor Novello Award for best selling A-side, won by Richard's Christmas single 'Mistletoe And Wine', 1988.

press day, shot a video for his next single, presented the 'Search For A Star' tennis awards and rehearsed at Pinewood Studios for his next tour.

His 30th anniversary tout was spread over September, October, November and December at the end of which his 99th single, Mistletoe and Wine was released. Following appearances on The Jimmy Tarbuck Show, Top Of The Pops and the Des O'Connor Show, the song went to No 1,

Jimmy Tarbuck also plays at Cliff's annual pro-celebrity tennis tournament alongside Aled Jones, Annabel Croft, Virginia Wade and Mike Read.

1989

After seeing-in the New Year in Perth, January began with Tear Fund and Arts Group meetings in Sydney, Melbourne and Wellington, a tennis tournament in Melbourne and a meeting with EMI executives in New Zealand.

On his return he recorded a song with Stock, Aitken and Waterman that had the working title of Harry but would become Just Don't Have The Heart.

He also added his backing vocals to the charity single, Everybody's Got A Crisis In Their Life.

In February, Cliff performed at The San Remo Song Festival, prior to appearing on Rome TV show, Europa, Europa and on Dutch TV.

On April 3rd, 2,000 fans were invited to the London Palladium where Cliff and Mike Read presented six of Cliff's new recordings for the fans to select their favourite, much as they did back in the early sixties when they chose Please Don't Tease. Stronger Than That came out on top, followed by Best Of Me and Just Don't Have The Heart.

As well as performing the six songs, Cliff also sang Bachelor Boy in memory of a long-term fan called Julie, who attended every show in her wheelchair.

Later in April, he attended the Ivor Novello Awards, the UK press day at EMI, saw the musicals Aspects Of Love and Metropolis and rehearsed for his next short-term residencies at Savvas Club in South Wales and Blazers at Windsor.

In May, Cliff was videoed discussing all his singles to date with Mike Read, opened a new radio studio at the local hospital and appeared on BBC TV's Going Live.

On May 30th Cliff's 100th single, Best Of Me was released and eventually reached No 2.

June 16th and 17th saw The Event taking place at Wembley Stadium, for which 14 cameras are used shooting 41 miles of film on a 400ft stage. Ninety artists took part in the show, which featured a total of 50 songs, Cliff, The Shadows, The Dallas Boys, The Kalin Twins, The Oh Boy Band, Jet Harris and Tony Meehan. Aswad were the special guest.

Two day later Cliff played in a pro-celebrity tennis tournament for the British Deaf Association in the presence of the Princess of Wales with Ivan Lendl, Michael Chang, Stefan Edberg, John Lloyd, Peter Fleming, Bruce Forsyth and Mike Read.

Four days later Cliff played in a tennis tournament in Holland before reading a lesson at Westminster Abbey for the Wishing Well appeal and attended Wimbledon where he watched Boris Becker beat Stefan Edberg in the men's final.

Cliff performed in Bonn as part of the city's 2,000th anniversary and received the Freedom of the City of London which allowed him to drive sheep over London Bridge and the privilege of being allowed to be hanged with a silk chord instead of a piece of rope (should the need arise!). He became the first person in the world of popular music to have the honour bestowed upon him.

In August, Cliff's 101st single Just Don't Have The Heart was released, the video having been shot on K stage at Shepperton Studios.

Promotion included UK appearances on The Sue Lawley Show, Roy Castle's Record Breakers and overseas appearances in Europe.

Cliff took a break in the US prior to the release of his next single, Lean On You, early in

Right: Cliff
accepting his
outstanding
contribution award
at the BRIT Awards
ceremony at the
Royal Albert Hall,
London, 18th
February 1989.

October. Promotion for this single included Top Of The Pops, the Des O'Connor Show, Motormouth and Record Breakers.

He performed on TV in Austria, Holland and Spain, before returning to launch the album Stronger at London's Trocadero with the help of strong man and former Olympic shot putter, Geoff Capes. The launch was followed by French and Swedish TV, a trip to Singapore and Japan and Belgian TV.

In November, Cliff presented veteran tennis player Fred Perry with an award, recorded LWT's New Year's Eve Show at the London Palladium, appeared on the Late, Late Show in Dublin and on French TV.

Early in December, Cliff and Van Morrison shot a video for their duet, Whenever God Shines His Light, at Shepperton Studios. The single would climb to No 20 in the chart and they would perform it at the ACG carol service at London's All Souls Church.

This year's pro-celebrity tennis tournament included Jason Donovan, Roy Castle and Virginia Wade.

1990

Early in January rehearsals began for the forthcoming February tour of Australia and New Zealand. A week into the tour, which lasted until the end of March, Cliff's 103rd single, Stronger Than That, was released, the song eventually peaking at No 14.

In April, Cliff attended the 'Search For A Star' launch to find new, young tennis players and began dance rehearsals for his forthcoming tour of Europe and Scandinavia.

The European tour ran from May 5th-June 7th, ending in Paris where he attended the French Open. In June, he went to the opening night of Mike Read's musical Young Apollo at the Thorndike Theatre, played celebrity tennis at David Lloyd's Club, attended the final of the Stella Artois tournament at Queen's Club and rehearsed with The Shadows for a concert at Knebworth.

The Knebworth Concert, in aid of the Nordoff-Robbins Music Therapy Clinic, also featured Pink Floyd, Status Quo, Paul McCartney, Elton John and Robert Plant and was broadcast 'live' on Radio One. Two of Cliff's tracks were used on Knebworth...The Album.

In the summer he performed for the Queen Mother's 90th birthday show at the London Palladium and his 104th single, Silhouettes, was released, making the top 10. The September schedule included TV rehearsals, and NEC concert rehearsals, before a week in cabaret in Usk, South Wales.

The week before the 105th single, From A Distance was released, Cliff shot a video for his Christmas single at Durdle Door near Lulworth Cove. To promote the current single he did interviews with DJs David Jensen and Graham Dene as well as performing on Going Live.

Cliff celebrated his 50th birthday at his home in Weybridge, asking guests to dress in 1950s clothes. Mike Read's group the Rock-olas performed during the evening, with Cliff joining them for some of his own songs and a version of Ricky Nelson's

Believe What You Say.

At midnight Cliff declared that he felt no different being 50: 'It was on my 50th birthday that I realised I didn't fear ageing. I said, "look nothing has changed." Everyone had been saying what a milestone 50 was, as though it was something to fear. I fear nothing any more.'

For his birthday he treated himself to a new Mercedes and gave each of his sisters £50,000.

In November, Cliff switched on the Oxford Street Christmas lights, appeared on BBC's Going Live and his 106th single, Saviour's Day was released. The song, a Chris Eaton number, gave Cliff another No 1.

In November, December and through to January 1991, Cliff played more than 40 dates on the From A Distance Tour, in Birmingham, Aberdeen, and Wembley Arena.

The annual pro-celebrity tennis tournament included Jeremy Irons, Paul Danials and Bruce Forsyth.

1991

Cliff opened the Harrods sale and in return, Mohammed Al Fayed donated £50,000 to the Daily Express Children of Chernobyl Appeal.

Three days later, Cliff attended a charity night for the Children of Chernobyl which raised £370,000 for the charity. Daily Express editor Sir Nicholas Lloyd presented Cliff with a painting by Russian artist Andrei Pakhomov.

The remainder of January saw Cliff working on his routine for the next gospel tour and holidaying in Florida.

The end of February and beginning of March was taken up with rehearsals for the gospel tour, which ran from March 13th to March 30th.

April brought meetings with director Frank Dunlop about the possibility of producing Wuthering Heights on stage, German TV shows and a pro-celebrity tennis tournament at Woking.

The social side of May included a reception at 10 Downing Street, the wedding of Warren Bennett – son of Shadows' drummer Brian Bennett, and an Everly Brothers concert at the Royal Albert Hall.

The business side took in the Ivor Novello Awards and the World Music Awards in Monte Carlo.

June was dominated by tennis, with a pro-celebrity match at the Royal Albert Hall, the final of the Stella Artois and Wimbledon, where Cliff watched Michael Stich beat Boris Becker in the men's final.

Having recorded More To Life, the theme song for the new TV series Trainer, he went to Sandown Park to watch some of the series being filmed, before attending the Federation Cup at Nottingham, where he appeared on the Radio One Roadshow and sat with the Princess of Wales for the opening ceremony of the ladies tennis tournament.

In August, Cliff holidayed in Portugal, before attending the opening night of the musical Oscar at Chilston Park in Kent.

September saw Cliff's first single release of the year, More To Life, his 107th single, which he performed on Top Of The Pops. The following day saw the publication of Peter Lewry and Nigel Goodall's book, The Complete Recording Sessions 1958-1990.

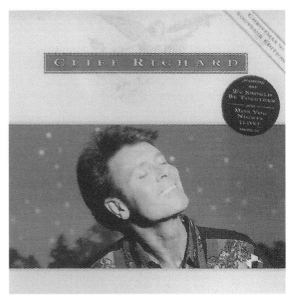

Cliff then undertook a week-long booking at Usk, before flying off to for a tour of Australia and New Zealand. Prior to his return, his 108th single, We Should Be Together was released, which he later performed on Top Of The Pops and the Des O'Connor Show.

His end of year pro-celebrity tennis tournament included, Des O'Connor, Bill Roache, Alvin Stardust, Mike Read and as usual, many top players.

Above: We Should Be Together, Christmas souvenir edition.

1992

The year began with the release of the single, This New Year, like Saviour's Day and Little Town, a Chris Eaton song.

Cliff undertook a 'sitting' for Rock Circus at Madame Tussaud's and attended the Saltmine event at the Royal Albert Hall before going skiing for the first time with a small group of friends at Lech in Austria.

Christian writer, Steve Turner began a new biography on Cliff to be published in the spring of 1993 and Cliff attended the opening night of Jack Good's musical, Good Rockin' Tonight, in which Cliff is portrayed by Timothy Whitnall.

Cliff's diary for February was an eclectic mix of Belgian and German TV, recording for BBC's Prayer of the Day, visiting Surrey schools, attending the premiere for Star Trek IV and watching Question Time at the House of Commons. The month ended with the launch of Cliff's 1992 Tennis Trail at Wimbledon and an impromptu performance with Wet Wet Wet on the TV show, Wogan.

March again, was a complete mixture, his diary recording the 'Spectacles Wearer of the Year' photocall, seeing Carmen Jones at the Old Vic, dining with actor

David Suchet, attending a Wet Wet Wet concert at Wembley and shoots for Bruce Forsyth's TV show.

At the end of March, Cliff returned to Lech for another skiing holiday and for the first time the Princess of Wales was there with the Princes William and Harry: 'Always on the final Friday night, Mike (Read) and I would sit with our guitars in the little bar after dinner and sing all the old songs together. We did it every year and it was good fun. Diana heard about the tradition and asked whether we would perform for William and Harry, so Mike and I joined them in the empty bar and sang all my hits. Harry asked for Great Balls Of Fire as it was one of his mother's favourites, so I sang it and Harry was beside himself with excitement. He grabbed a Toblerone packet that was lying on the table and using it as a microphone, gyrated like Michael Jackson while Mike and I did the number. William meanwhile sat back and just moved his arms a little…and remained totally cool. I will remind him that my first Royal

Command performance for him was at Lech. It was fun and all the more enjoyable for knowing that the paparazzi were massed outside the hotel that night, blissfully unaware of the good time we were having inside.'

On his return his time was taken up recording at RG Jones studio and he spendt many evenings at the theatre including another visit to Jack Good's Good Rockin' Tonight, Mike Read's Poetry In Motion, Tim Rice and Andrew Lloyd Webber's Jesus Christ Superstar and attended the ballet at Sadler's Wells.

In the spring Cliff and Bill Latham flew to Uganda to shoot a documentary for Tear Fund, before appearing on Danish TV and recording for Gloria Hunniford's TV show. An appearance at the World Music Awards with Olivia Newton–John is followed by French TV, promotion work in Paris and the French Open.

Prior to tennis at Queen's Club, Cliff dined with veteran tennis commentator, Dan Maskell and then attended his own tennis trail, during which he was interviewed by John Motson.

June saw Cliff attending the musical, Oscar, in Oxford, taking part in a Sammy Davis tribute evening and opening the BBC's National Music Day, singing Move It from the roof of Broadcasting House.

During the summer he attended more tennis trail events, holidayed in Portugal and appeared in a week-long residency at Usk, which was a curtain raiser for a 42-date tour of the UK and Dublin.

Cliff's new single, I Still Believe In You was released in November, the CD single including Ocean Deep. He performed it on Pebble Mill and Wogan, is interviewed for Radio One by Simon Bates and sings at Joy To The World which is shot for Christmas transmission by the BBC.

The pro-celebrity tennis tournament moved from Brighton to Birmingham as it entered its 10th year; players including Frank Bruno, Michael Ball, Roy Castle and Gloria Hunniford attended.

Left: Cliff
performed for
Diana, William
and Harry during
a skiing holiday in
Lech.

1993, 1994 & 1995

Early in the year, Cliff was back skiing with friends in Lech before releasing his new single, Peace In Our Time, a double video, Access All Areas – The Tour 1992 and starting a 13-date gospel tour of the UK.

In April, Cliff Richard the Album entered the UK chart at No 1 as the Access All Areas double video entered the video chart at No 1.

The Christmas release of 1993 was a re-working of the Everly Brothers' No1, All I Have To Do Is Dream coupled with Miss You Nights.

On October 25th 1995, Cliff became the first British rock star to be knighted. Bob Geldof had received his honorary knighthood nine years earlier, but not being a British subject, he was not permitted to use the title 'Sir', whether in the UK or abroad. Knighthoods would later follow for Paul McCartney, Elton John, Mick Jagger and Tom Jones.

The autumn of 1995 saw the release of the first single from the musical Heathcliff, Misunderstood Man, which just made the top 20.

The second release from the musical, Had To Be, came out in December reaching No 22.

1996

March 1996 saw the release of The Wedding from Heathcliff, the single just making the top 40.

One of the strangest and most memorable highlights of Cliff's career occurred during Wimbledon fortnight. Rain, as always was causing problems which meant a delay to the men's quarter-final between Pete Sampras and Richard Krajicek in which the scores were level at 2-2. In the members enclosure, Jennifer, the wife of Chief Executive Chris Gorringe suggested that the Centre Court crowd might enjoy hearing Cliff sing, to keep them entertained during the rain delay. A message was sent down to Cliff who was being interviewed on Radio Wimbledon and the scene was set for what Cliff would call, 'The most unusual performance of my career.'

He kicked off with Summer Holiday followed by The Young Ones, during which he was joined by a tribe of the lady tennis players, which included Virginia Wade, Martina Navratilova, Pam Shriver, Gigi Fernandez and Conchita Martinez. Cliff then announced that they had formed a group called Cliff and the Supremes as the backing singers are all tennis supremos! They stayed with him for the rest of the impromptu gig, which included Bachelor Boy, All Shook Up, Living Doll, and Congratulations.

The spectacle was witnessed by Prince & Princess Michael of Kent and Royal Box guest Joanna Lumley.

Right: Cliff
orchestrates the
singing as the
crowd join in
on another rain
delayed days
play during the
Wimbledon tennis
championships
at the all England
club in London.

Unaware that the BBC still had their cameras rolling and after singing six of his golden greats, TV presenter Des Lynam commented on this and added jokingly 'we'll probably get one hell of a bill'. The performance was front-page headlines on many of the major British newspapers the following day, some even suggesting that it was a premeditated PR stunt.

Interviewed at a later date about the day he said: 'I happened to be there that day and because it was raining I was asked to do an interview with Radio Wimbledon, who had a little studio on Centre Court. After about 20 minutes someone came in and said that the club secretary wanted a word with me. Being my first year as a member, my immediate assumption was that I must have done something wrong. But when I went up to see him, he told me his wife had suggested that he ask me to sing something. I said I couldn't really – I didn't have a guitar, and I wasn't sure how it would work. So he suggested I just do an interview instead, for the Centre Court crowd. I said that'll be fine. But at the end of the interview the guy turned to the audience and said: "Before I let you go, they would never forgive me if I don't ask you to sing." Well, I'm a professional. If I'm put on the spot, I can't really say no.'

1997, 1998 & 1999

Be With Me Always was Cliff's only hit that year, failing to make the top 50, peaking at 52.

In 1998, annoyed that many radio stations were refusing to play his records, Cliff released Can't Keep This Feeling In on a white label under the pseudonym of Black Knight. The name was dreamed up through him being a Knight of the realm and the producer being Clive Black. The single was well regarded and featured on playlists until the true artist was revealed. Nevertheless it made the top 10.

June 1998 saw Cliff appearing on TFI Friday.

The first of Cliff's two 1999 hits was The Miracle, released at the beginning of August, reaching the top 30.

Controversy again arose with regard to radio stations refusing to play his records when EMI, Cliff's label since 1958, refused to release his latest song, Millennium Prayer. Cliff took it to an independent label, Papillon, who released the charity recording (in aid of Children's Promise). The single topped the UK chart for three weeks, becoming his 14th No 1 and the third-highest-selling single of his career. Well done EMI!

2000

He learns that the Caribbean is commemorating him with a special stamp, a spokeswoman for the Antigua and Barbuda High Commission saying, 'Sir Cliff had a huge following on the islands. The people of Antigua and Barbuda love the music of Sir Cliff and I'm not surprised he is getting his own stamp.'

Cliff says that he is "shocked and honoured." An amazed Sir Cliff, who is celebrating four decades at the top of the charts, said he did not realise he had so many fans around the world. He told on newspaper: "It is a strange feeling to have a stamp made out of your picture but I feel it is a great honour and perhaps I should take a trip down to the Caribbean to say thank you.

"I can't believe that there will be hundreds of letters being posted around the world with my face on." The $1.65 Caribbean stamp shows Sir Cliff in relaxed mood wearing a dark jacket and white open-neck shirt.

Coincidentally Cliff buys a plot of land on the west coast of Barbados and commissions a six-bedroom house to be built on it. Cliff would later reflect: 'I really like Barbados. I love the heat and pace of life and the sociability of it.'

His vineyard is doing so well that he is able to produce two or three hundred bottles of wine. The BBC features The Cliff Richard Story and the South Bank Show give him a lifetime achievement award.   In October 2000 Cliff takes

60 friends on a Mediterranean cruise to celebrate his 60th birthday on the 343 ton Seaburn Goddess. The cruise begins at Nice and sails to St Tropez, Monte Carlo, Barcelona and Palma, but is unable to go to Italy because of bad weather.

Guests include Olivia Newton-John, Shadows Bruce Welch and Brian Bennett, Tim Rice, Sue Barker, Gloria Hunniford, Bobby Davro, John Farrar and Mike Read, all of whom perform at some point during the trip.

Tennis is very much on the agenda, with matches in Barcelona, St Tropez and La Residencia in Mallorca.

During the cruise, Cliff's keyboard player gets married on board ship, with the Rev Garth Hewitt officiating and Cliff giving the bride away and singing How Great Thou Art.

OK Magazine produced a special magazine and DVD of the event, having been allowed exclusively on board while the ship was docked at Monte Carlo.

Cliff said; I didn't invite my sister jacqui and her family because they're Jehovah's Witnesses (who don't celebrate birthdays.) I didn't invite Hamk Marvin for the saem reason. Almost everyone I cared about was there and on the night of my birthday we had a big party in Monte Carlo.

2001

Far Right: Cliff
arrives at the
Television & Radio
Industries Club
(TRIC) Awards
March 12, 2002.

Richard's next album, in 2001, was a covers project, Wanted, produced by Alan Tarneyfollowed by another top ten album, Cliff at Christmas. The holiday album contained both new and older recordings, including the single Santa's List which would reach No. 5 in 2003.

His re-working of Somewhere Over The Rainbow/What a Wonderful World had been suggested to him by DJ Graham Dene who was thought Hawaiin singer Israel Kamakawiwo'ole's version of the medley would be ideal for Cliff to cover. The song peaked just outside the top ten.

Cliff sells the very first bottles of his own wine, which he has called Vida Nova.

In May he performs at the Royal Albert Hall and on a TV special, The Hits I Missed, before spending time in Portugal, France, the Usa and Barbados where work begins on his new house.

In November the DVD Unforgettable is released and Cliff appears on The Frank Skinner Show, The Hits I Missed and The Way We were.

2002

Cliff's only hit of 2002 is Let Me Be The One which just made the top thirty, but he is voted by the public 56th in the Greatest Britons poll sponsored by the BBC.

In April Cliff appears on Des O'Connor Meets Cliff Richard

Cliff spends some time in Portugal overseeing his wine crop, which yields 27,000 bottles of Vida Nova.

In June Cliff performs for HM The Queen's Jubilee Concert which is shown on TV as BBC's Party At The Palace.

November saw the start of the UK leg of a world tour with fans camping out for days, to make sure that they obtained tickets.

2003

Cliff Richard finished number 56 in the 2002 100 Greatest Britons list, sponsored by the BBC and voted for by the public.

He's also honoured by Portugal as Rua da Caviera in Albufeira is to be re-named Rua da Cliff Richard, much to the delight of the residents as their road previously meant 'skull street.'

Early in the year Cliff...The Musical begins a UK tour and stars Jimmy Jemain, Mike Read, Ricky Aron and Gordon Kenny. The show, set in the year 2020, features the songs of Cliff and is directed by Trevor Payne, the star of touring show, That'll Be The Day. The tour ends with a run in the West End at The Prince of Wales Theatre.

Cliff receives an award from the Lawn Tennis Association for twenty years of service to tennis and is also awarded a Gold Badge by the British Academy of Composers and Authors.

This year sees the release of three DVDs, Live In The Park, World Tour 2003, The Countdown Concert and Cliff Richard Featuring The Shadows.

In the autumn Cliff performs at a gala festival for a German radio station in Cologne.

Cliff's Christmas single is Santa's List which makes the top five.

2004

In February Cliff appears on The Ultimate Pop Star.

Cliff went to to Nashville, Tennessee for his next album project, employing a writers' conclave to give him the pick of all new songs for the album Something's Goin' On. Though the collection was critically well-received, it had disappointing sales. Nevertheless it was yet another top ten album, and produced three top fifteen singles: "Something's Goin' On" and "I Cannot Give You My Love", written by Barry Gibb of the Bee Gees, (both released in 2004)and the driving "What Car" which would be released the following year. Cliff did not hide his disappointment with the album's lacklustre sales, and it was speculated that it might have been his last ever album of original songs.

He joins The Shadows on stage at the London Palladium for what is assumed to be their last appearance performing together.

Cliff is inducted into the UK Music Hall of Fame and also becomes joint owner of Manchester's Arora International Hotel.

In October Cliff appears on Parkinson and Ant and Dec's Saturday Night Takeaway and the DVD Live (Castles In The Air) is released.

December sees Cliff appearing on The Royal Variety Performance and Top Gear.

2005

Cliff spends the early part of the year in Barbados, where he sings at a charity concert for athe Barbados Children's Trust.

Harrods is the venue for the launch and photocall for the new album, Somethin' Is Going On.

In May 2005 Cliff appears on BBC 1's A Party To Remember, and also opens the new radio station BIG L, the successor to the old pirate station, Radio London. The station opens with the same song the original station began with, I Could Easily Fall, followed by Cliff's new single, What Car. Cliff arrives at the station in a double-decker bus, does the opening hour with Mike Read and poses for photographs with the Cheeky Girls.

He later attends the new the latest Star Wars film.

Cliff sings at the VE day Concert in Trafalgar Square.

August sees Cliff performing at the Building One World festival in Cologne after the Concluding Mass of World Youth Day.

In the autumn Cliff is inducted into the Avenue of Stars in Covent Garden (all the stars being removed the following year due to deterioration) and the Pride Of Britain Awards.

A clutch of DVDs are released in October; Live In The Park, The 40th Anniversary Concerts and The Countdown Concert.

Cliff's wine, Vida Nova2004 wins a bronze medal at the 2005 London wine Fair.

At the end of the year Cliff attends the world premiere for The Chronicles of Narnia, hosts his pro-celebrity tennis tournament at the NEC Birmingham and appears on the The Royal Variety Performance.

Above: Cliff performs at A Party To Remember, a free concert celebrating the 60th anniversary of VE Day, in Trafalgar Square, London

2006

In April, Cliff boards the Nationwide routemaster bus in London's Docklands, which is en-route to Germany in time for the FIFA 2006 World Cup. The bus will tour towns across the UK and will be signed by celebrity well-wishers. "The Nationwide England Fans' Bus will also provide entertainment throughout the tournament in Germany and be taken to goodwill events between the England supporters, the German hosts and other nations.

In June Cliff appears on the 11th episode of Gordon Ramsay's TV Show, The F Word, after which the chef claimed that Cliff swore at him, having been tricked into damning his own wine.

Cliff appears on the BBC 1 TV show, The Queen at 80 and later attends her celebrations at St Paul's Cathedral.

Portugal honours him with their version of a knighthood to acknowledge forty years of personal and business involvement with the country.

In a September 2006 interview with the Daily Mail, Cliff speaks about the difficulties he and his sisters had in dealing with their mother's condition as she was suffering from dementia.

At the end of October, Cliff releases a version of Yesterday Once More, duetting with Irish singer Daniel O'Donnell who cites his all-

time favourite song as Cliff's Miss You Nights.

The single is taken from Two's Company, an album of duets released in 2006, was another top 10 success and also included newly-recorded material with Brian May, Dionne Warwick, Anne Murray, Barry Gibb as well as previously recorded duets with artists such as Phil Everly, Elton John and Olivia Newton-John.

Two's Company was released to coincide with the UK leg of his latest world tour, Here and Now, which included My Kinda Life, How Did She Get Here, Hey Mr. Dream Maker", For Life, A Matter Of Moments, When The Girl In Your Arms, Every Face Tells A Story, Peace In Our Time.

Cliff's wine Vida Nova, is awarded a Silver medal at the International Spirit and Wine Fair and the Here and NowLive DVD is released.

In November, Cliff becomes the second artist to unveil a plaque of their handprints for the Wembley Sqare of Fame. Madonna had previously unveiled hers.

21st Century Christmas is released and backed by a new version of Move It, featuring Brian May and Brian Bennett. The single reached No. 2 on the UK singles chart and is helped by Cliff appearing twice on the TV programme, Strictly Come Dancing.

2007

Cliff's perfume range now includes, Dream Maker, Devil Woman and Miss You Nights.

In Paris, Cliff duets on Summer Holiday with David Gest for the ITV show, This Is David Gest.

Cliff is one of many singers that advocated extending music copyright from fifty to seventy years, as his recordings would soon become available for any record label to use without paying any fees.

US music copyright royalties last for ninety-five years.

The Who's Roger Daltrey, whose first works will go out of copyright in seven years, says that musicians "enriched people's lives", and that they were "not asking for a handout, just a fair reward for their creative endeavours". He also complained that artists had "no pensions and rely on royalties".

Tory leader David Cameron is also a member of the extensionist camp.

The Government review concluded that an extension would not benefit the majority of performers, most of whom have contractual relationships requiring their royalties be paid back to the record label," said ministers.

The government disagreed with the artists, citing the independent

Gowers Review in which ex-Financial Times editor Andrew Gowers probed the issue.

"[Gowers] considered not just the impact on the music industry but on the economy as a whole, and concluded that an extension would lead to increased costs to industry, such as those who use music – whether to provide ambience in a shop or restaurant or for TV or radio broadcasting – and to consumers... the review took account of the question of parity with other countries such as the US, and concluded that, although royalties were payable for longer there, the total amount was likely to be similar – or possibly less – as there were fewer revenue streams available under the US system."

Another compilation album, Love... The Album was released on 12 November 2007. Like Two's Company before it, this album includes both previously released material and newly recorded songs, namely Waiting For A Girl Like You, When You Say Nothing At All, All Out Of Love, If You're

Left: Cliff arrives for the Service of Thanksgiving for the life of Diana, Princess of Wales, at the Guards' Chapel, in London, 31 August 2007.

Not the One and When I Need You. The latter song was released as a single, just making the top forty, despite promoting it on the Alan Titchmarsh Show and This Morning. The album peaks at number 13, but the concept of the project has divided fans who had anticipated an album of new material.

In October, Cliff's mother Dorothy, who has suffered from dementia for years, dies at eighty-seven.

In December, Cliff appears on The Paul O'Grady Show, The One Show and Strictly Come Dancing.

2008

2008 is Cliff's 50th year in the music business, the anniversary seeing the release of the 8 CD box set And They Said It Wouldn't Last (My 50 Years In Music)

Early in the year Cliff appears on the BBC TV tribute programme to Bruce Forsyth, Happy Birthday Brucie, and takes part in a charity walk on the great wall of China for Olivia Newton John's cancer centre.

On the social front, Cliff attends the Cannes Film Festival and The Champions Dinner at Wimbledon.

In September, The Variety Club give a 50th anniversary lunch for Cliff and he releases a single celebrating his 50 years in pop music, titled "Thank you for a Lifetime which he promotes on The One Show. On 14 September 2008 it reached No. 3 on the UK music charts. The same month Cliff's new book My Life, My Way, co-written with Penny Junor, is published which Cliff dedictaes to, 'My Mum and Dad, who are now reunited, and who were an even greater influence on me than Elvis and to all my fans who have stuck by me through the years.' He signs copies at Waterstones in London's Piccadilly, Lakeside and The Trafford Centre, Manchester and performs at the Woolworth's Red Carpet Bash to clebrate his 50 years in show business.

A special edition of the Time

Machine Tour DVD is released.

In October Cliff gives a 50th Anniversary Fan Club Tea for presidents of his fan club and editors of Cliff magazines and websites, at Oakley Court Hotel in Windsor. He answers questions, chats about his life and times with Bill Latham and gives everyone present a commemorative 50th anniversary key ring, which includes fans have travelled for the occasion from as far afield as South Africa, the USA, Australia and New Zealand.

In the autumn, Cliff becomes a patron of the Alzheimer's Research Trust and makes a plea on their behalf on BBC TV.

On 2 November British newspaper The Mail on Sunday gave away a free promotional CD entitled 50th Anniversary containing 12 tracks selected by Sir Cliff himself.

On 11 November Cliff Richard's official website announced that 20 years after their latest concert together, Cliff and The Shadows would reunite to celebrate their 50th anniversary in the music business. A month later they perform at the Royal Variety Performance and Cliff appears on The Paul O'Grady Show.

Cliff's Time Machine UK tour runs from November 10th to 2nd December and takes in Wembley, Cardiff, Birmingham, Manchester, Newcastle, Glasgow and Belfast.

Above: Cliff arrives at the 2008 Wimbledon Champions Dinner

2009

In June 2009 it was reported by Sound Kitchen Studios in Nashville that Cliff was to return there shortly to record a new album of original recordings of jazz songs. He was to record fourteen tracks in a week. He also stated his intention to record with bluegrass singer Alison Krauss.

In the late summer, Cliff releases what will become his 135th hit single and 124th top 40 hit, Singing The Blues, taken from the new Cliff & the Shadows album, Reunited. To date he has had 62 hit albums, 67 top 10 hit singles, 47 top 20 hits and 55 top 40 hits.

Prior to the major tour, Piers Morgan interviews Cliff at his home in Barbados for the ITV show, When Piers Met Cliff, in which he also took Cliff back to his old home in Cheshunt.

In September, Cliff and the Shadows release a new album, Reunited, their first studio project together for forty years. The 28 tracks recorded comprise 25 re-recordings of their earlier classics, with three "new" tracks, originally from the late 1950's Singing the Blues, Eddie Cochran's C'mon Everybody Frankie Ford's Sea Cruise.

The album charted at number

6 in the UK charts in its opening week and peaked at number 4.

The same month he appears on The Paul O'Grady Show and The One Show, and along with the Shadows, sign copies of their DVD at HMV Oxford Street.

Cliff and The Shadows re-unite to undertake a massive tour that takes in the UK, Australia, New Zealand, Europe and South Africa and runs into 2010.

On December 8th Cliff hosts the annual Tennis Foundation evening at Hampton Court, which this year features Brain Conley, Dame Evelyn Glennie and The London Community Gospel Choir.

Above: Cliff and The Shadows performs live on stage at the O2 Arena on September 28, 2009.

2010

The Reunited tour continues in New Zealand, Australia and South Africa.

In April 2010, Cliff's girlfriend from 1960 and 1961, Delia Wicks dies of cancer.

The same month sees Cliff's Vida Nova featured on Oz Clarke's on-line wine tasting which gives a large number of people the chance to judge six Portuguese wines, Rare and Unseen DVD become his 40th hit on the DVD/Video chart and he sings Congratulations at the 70th birthday celebrations of Queen Margrethe II of Denmark. Cliff is able to catch one of the last flights back to Barbados before the UK air space ban is implemented due to volcanic ash.

Cliff attends a gala dinner at the Dorchester as his fans pay tribute to his career and birthday. Singers Simon Goodall and Jimmy Jemain both entertain the fans and Cliff joins Simon for a surprise duet on Miss You Nights.

In October, Cliff's new album, Bold As Brass is released, having been produced in Nashville by

Grammy-Award-winning Christian musician, Michael Omartian, who has also produced such artists as Steely Dan, The Jacksons, Whitney Houston, Rod Stewart, Michael Bolton and Christopher Cross. The album includes such classics as Lazy River, Night & Day, Let's Fall In Love, and I've Got You Under My Skin, and is accompanied by a week at the Albert Hall from 11th-17th October.

The phrase Bold as Brass comes from the London Mayor of 1770, Brass Crosby, who courageously took on the House of Commons, for which he was thrown on the Tower, before being forgiven. The phrase has lasted 240 years and has now been brought back to life by Cliff in 2010.

At the end of October Cliff throws a 70th birthday bash for his friends at a prestigious hotel near Heathrow.

Above: Cliff and The Shadows during one of their reunion tour shows.

2011

The highlight of 2011 was the Soulicious album and tour. On the fifteen track CD Cliff sang with a whole galaxy of top soul stars; Freda Payne, Dennis Edwards & The Temptations Review, Brenda Holloway, Candi Staton, Roberta Flack, Deniece Williams, Marilyn McCoo & Billy Davis Jnr, Valeria Simpson, Russell Thompkins Jnr & The New Stylistics, Lamont Dozier, Percy Sledge, Billy Paul, and Peabo Bryson. The album peaked at No10 in the UK album Chart.

Cliff's ensuing sell-out UK tour featured Percy Sledge, Marilyn McCoo and Billy Davis Jnr, James Ingram, Lamont Dozier and Jaki Graham.

2012

On June 4th 2012 Cliff performed on the specially constructed stage around the Queen Victoria Memorial for HM The Queen's Diamond Jubilee Concert. Organised by Take That's Gary Barlow, the show also featured such luminaries as Paul McCartney, Tom Jones, Elton John and Shirley Bassey.

Cliff ostensibly performed songs from the six decades in which he's had hits, but the more observant fans will have spotted two from the seventies (Devil Woman and We Don't Talk Anymore) and none from the eighties. Rather unusually he began with Dynamite, the B Side of Travelling Light, which also charted in it's own right. Many were surprised that he didn't open with his first hit single, Move It. The Young Ones, Millennium Prayer and Congratulations completed his six-minute, energetic set.

Watched by 15 million people across the UK, the concert was also enjoyed by 18,000 watching it in front of Buckingham Palace.

Left: Cliff performs on stage during the Diamond Jubilee concert at Buckingham Palace on June 4th, 2012.

Not simply flying in for the high profile Diamond Jubilee Concert, Cliff also continues to appear right across the spectrum, as he always has; this visit, supporting Shooting Star CHASE, of which he has been a patron since 2003. At their Hampton Hospice he joined a string quartet to entertain the children and adults. Following his visit, during which he performed Summer Holiday, Cliff said: "As patron of Shooting Star CHASE, hospice care for children and teenagers, my visit to Shooting Star House was such an inspiration. To see the courage of life-limited children and the love and wonderful dedication of the staff, carers and volunteers puts so much of life into perspective."

ALSO AVAILABLE IN THE LITTLE BOOK SERIES

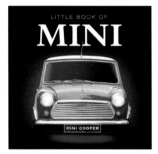

ALSO AVAILABLE IN THE LITTLE BOOK SERIES

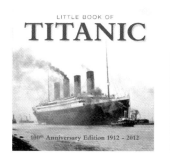

The pictures in this book were provided courtesy of the following:

GETTY IMAGES
101 Bayham Street, London NW1 0AG

WIKIMEDIA COMMONS

Design and artwork by: Scott Giarnese

Published by: G2 Entertainment Limited

Publishers: Jules Gammond and Edward Adams

Written by: Mike Read